EVOLUTION OF STUPAS IN BURMA
Pagan Period: 11th to 13th centuries A.D.

BUDDHIST TRADITIONS

Edited by
ALEX WAYMAN

VOLUME XII

EVOLUTION OF STUPAS IN BURMA

Pagan Period: 11th to 13th centuries A.D.

SUJATA SONI

MOTILAL BANARSIDASS PUBLISHERS PVT. LTD.
DELHI

First Edition: 1991

Also available at
MOTILAL BANARSIDASS
Chowk, Varanasi 221 001
Ashok Rajpath, Patna 800 004
16 St. Mark's Road, Bangalore 560 001
120 Royapettah High Road, Mylapore, Madras 600 004
41 U.A. Bungalow Road, Jawahar Nagar, Delhi-110 007

ISBN: 81-208-0626-3

PRINTED IN INDIA
BY JAINENDRA PRAKASH JAIN AT SHRI JAINENDRA PRESS, A-45 NARAINA INDUSTRIAL AREA, PHASE I, NEW DELHI 110028 AND PUBLISHED BY NARENDRA PRAKASH JAIN FOR MOTILAL BANARSIDASS PUBLISHERS PVT. LTD., BUNGALOW ROAD, JAWAHAR NAGAR, DELHI 110007

Affectionately Dedicated
To the Memory of My Beloved Father
Dr. RUP LAL SONI

In Saṁsāra countless times have we met,
Each repaying the other's debt,
Truth, the common goal, our quest,
Till in Nibbāna we eternally rest.

Foreword by Series Editor

Miss Sujata Soni's work on the Burmese Stūpas will doubtless help fill a void of information on the architecture of the Eastern side of the Himalayas. The classic work by A.H. Longhurst, *The Story of the Stūpa*, deals with Himalaya architecture only from Kashmir to Nepal. Inspired by her father's interest in Burmese history, Miss Soni undertook the studies herein presented for a Master of Arts degree at Mandalay, Burma, in 1969. She exhibits greater maturity than would be expected for a modest academic degree, in combining the various fragments of data from the Pagan period (11th to 13th centuries), starting soon after the arrival of the modern Burmese people in the area called Burma.

Since such monuments of the Himalaya area have been subject to much natural and human spoilage in recent years, Miss Soni's work may help preserve, at least on the literary level, the memory of a once-glorious period of architectural creativity. It is therefore a pleasure to include her work in the Buddhist Traditions Series.

ALEX WAYMAN

Foreword

Pagan, the early Burmese capital, is well-known as a unique historic site where thousands of monuments still stand in different stages of preservation, testifying the cultural development of the glorious city. These edifices had deteriorated much through the ravages of time and occasional earthquakes as well as human vandalism. Yet, among the surviving monuments and ruins of structures there remain ample materials for the study of the vestiges of Burmese art, iconography and architecture. In fact, the wealth of materials is so vast that whatever had been published on Pagan amounts to just a portion of the inexhaustible research opportunities open to scholars in the field of art, archaeology and epigraphy.

Miss Sujata Soni has grasped the opportunity of studying meticulously one aspect of Pagan culture, viz., the evolution of stupas. By dint of diligent research and painstaking observations she has achieved her goal in submitting her thesis for the post-graduate degree in History. Her work is not confined to the technical appreciation of the architectural evolution of stupas at Pagan. She discusses the philosophical issues raised by the erection of the multitude of stupas, draws comparisons with neighbouring countries and considers the significance of the Pagan stupa designed and adopted to conform to Burmese conceptions. These facts reflect Miss Soni's original thinking and enhance the value of her book which turns out to be not only informative and readable but extremely thought provoking. It will prove useful to scholars for its detailed references and profuse illustrations. I earnestly look forward to the early publication of her work.

AUNG THAW
Director-General
Department of Archaeology
Ministry of Culture

Rangoon
December 9, 1980

Prologue

This work was a thesis for Master of Arts Degree from the Arts and Science University in Mandalay (Burma), in 1969. It deals with the evolutionary phases in the Buddhist solid shrines in Burma between the 11th and 13th centuries. Besides, it details a comparative study of the contemporary state of Buddhist architecture in Asia. Moreover, the study goes back to the burial mounds in the Vedic Period in Indian history and goes ahead to the final stage in the evolution of the solid pagodas as represented in the Shwedagon Shrine in Rangoon (Burma).

The evolutionary phase in the architecture of solid pagodas, has, unfortunately, so far received only fragmentary attention. This phase, which is of importance in the field of Burmese art, needs to be studied from different angles. The material side of the subject has received quite a consideration in this thesis. Obviously, observations on the physical side of the theme are not enough. There is, besides, the need of looking into the aesthetic and the spiritual aspects of the evolution.

The fact is that every phase forward in the architectural evolution of the solid pagodas was marked by a progressive and positive move not only in the aesthetic sense but also in the sense of the spiritual values. It was thus that the impressiveness of the structure in the physical sense became but a part of its beauty in the spiritual sense. In this way, the national psychology found its true expression in the visible objectification of the worldly and religious aspirations lurking in the Burmese mind. No wonder, that the actual life of the people is known by an admirable synthesis of the worldly and other-worldly aspirations, and the Burmese pagoda in its finalized form is truly symbolic of the natural disposition of the people, who while quite fond of worldly pleasures are not forgetful of the transcendental objective of human existence. Such an intuitional synthesis does much credit to the people.

Certainly, present-day Pagan, eloquent of the socio-economic well-being of the people and religious zeal of the Period, abounds in sermons in stone, brick and mortar. Though in ruins, it gives the impression of a grand landscape on the banks of the majestic Irrawaddy river. Bathed in the light of the sun from above and washed by the ripples of the river on its side, Pagan was veritably a fairyland on earth. The visitor today instinctively conjures up the grand vision of its past glory, with numerous gorgeous shrines, vast monasteries, great libraries and royal apartments, full of life, religious devotion and cultural splendour.

Abstract

This thesis is centred round the study of the evolutionary phases which the *cetī* or the stupa architecture underwent in Burma during the Pagan dynasty from the 11th to the 13th centuries. The subject is discussed in its historical setting. The indigenous styles at Pagan are found emerging from the models in pre-*Aniruddha* Pagan and also at the earlier Pyu centre at *Śrī Kṣetra,* which in turn are discovered with influences harking back to India.

One of the special contributions of our study is to emphasize that though the *cetī* architecture is basically outlandish, the finalization of its evolution in Burma was the outcome of the Burmese genius during the Pagan period. Certain specific architectural features initiated by the Burmese in the building of *cetī* are detailed and established as a unique contribution of the Pagan period to the Buddhist art in particular and to the world of art in general. Moreover, the subject of the evolution of the *cetī* architecture in Burma is dealt with in a way with original touch to the subject.

Another contribution of this study is the presentation of certain philosophical views on the subject and the refutation of certain ideas lacking rational basis. Moreover, certain architectural problems presented by the encased stupas are discussed in the light of the available material. And, finally, the comparative study of the contemporary religious architecture in the neighbouring countries offers new ideas, which can well become the basis of the revival of the cultural unity of Asia.

An art section is added. It provides a pictorial presentation which facilitates the entire study. Besides, it gives a realistic view of the form and style of architecture unique to each shrine.

Contents

Transliteration Table

1. Consonants

က ka	စ ca	ဋ ṭa	တ ta	ပ pa	ယ ya	သ sa
ခ kha	ဆ cha	ဌ ṭha	ထ tha	ဖ pha	ရ ra	ဟ ha
ဂ ga	ဇ ja	ဍ ḍa	ဒ da	ဗ ba	လ la	ံ ṁ
ဃ gha	ဈ jha	ဎ ḍha	ဓ dha	ဘ bha	ဠ ḷa	အ a
င ṅa	ဉ ña	ဏ ṇa	န na	မ ma	ဝ wa	

For various forms of sa: śa, ṣa, sa, ssa

2. Vowels

a, အာ ā, ဣ i, ဤ ī, ဥ u, ဦ ū

e, e', e.

o, ò, ó, ô

3. Combinations

ိ i	ီ ī	ု u	ူ ū	ေ e	ော o	ို ui
ဲ ai	ော် au	ျ y	ြ r	ွ w	ှ h	
k	င် ṅ	စ် c	တ် t	ပ် p	ဉ် ñ	- ဿ or ဿ

4. Numerals

၁ 1 ၂ 2 ၃ 3 ၄ 4 ၅ 5 ၆ 6 ၇ 7 ၈ 8 ၉ 9 ၀ 0

5. Other signs (frequently used for land measure)

«	½	ခွဲ	khwai
+	¼	စိတ်	cit
		စ ရွတ်	carwat
		ဟု / ဖု	hu or phu
		ပြည်	prañ
		လမယ်	lamay

---

1. See also JBRS, IV, ii, 136; JBRS, VI, ii, p. 81-90 & Ep. Birm., I, i, pp. 6-12

List of Abbreviations

<u>ခေတ်ဟောင်း</u>	သန်းထွန်း၊ <u>ခေတ်ဟောင်း မြန်မာရာဇဝင်</u>၊ (ရန်ကုန် မဟာဒဂုံ စာပေ ထုတ်ဝေရေး၊ ၁၉၆၄)
<u>ပဒေသာ</u>	စိန်မောင်ဦး၊ "သရေခေတ္တရာမြို့ဟောင်း"၊ <u>ပညာပဒေသာ</u>၊ ရန်ကုန်၊ အတွဲ ၃၊ အပိုင်း ၁၊ ဇန်နဝါရီ၊ ၁၉၆၈၊ စာမျက်နှာ ၁၆၃–၂၀၉
ABCJA	*ABC of Japanese Art* (Tokyo, Board of Tourist Industry, 1937)
AHI	Majumdar, Raychaudhuri & Datta: *An Advanced History of India*, (New York, St. Martin's Press, 1965)
AM	*The Annual Magazine*, Mandalay University
ASB	Annual Report of the Superintendent, Archaeological Survey, Burma
ASI	Annual Report of the Superintendent, Archaeological Survey, India
AT	Bowie, Theodore (ed): *The Arts of Thailand*, (Bloomington, Indiana University Press, 1960)
BK	U Bo Ke
BRMNT	*Burma Review and Monday New Times*, Rangoon
BRSFAP II	*Burma Research Society Fiftieth Anniversary Publication*, Number Two
BWS	Karunaratne, T.B.: *The Buddhist Wheel Symbol*, (Kandy, Buddhist Publication Society, 1969)
C	*Cheingmai*, (Bangkok, Nai Sura Saranakhom, 1966)
DC	*Dagabas of Ceylon*, (Kandy, Buddhist Publication Society, 1967)
F	*Forward*, (Rangoon, Ministry of Information, published bimonthly since 1962)
GM	*The Guardian Magazine*, Rangoon

HA	Chamanlal: *Hindu America,* (Hoshiarpur, Dev Datt Shastri, 1956)
HBB	Than Tun: *History of Buddhism in Burma (Pagan Period),* (Rangoon People's Literature Publications, 1962)
HIEA	Fergusson, James: *History of Indian and Eastern Architecture,* I & II, (Delhi, Munshiram Manoharlal, 1967)
IA	Brown, Percy: *Indian Architecture (Buddhist & Hindu),* (Bombay, Taraporevala Sons & Co. Ltd., 1942)
IAC	Sen, A. C. (ed): *The Indo-Asian Culture*
IET	*Indonesia Economy and Tourism,* Djakarta
IM	*The India Magazine*
JA	Shinkokai, K.B.: *Japanese Architecture III,* (Tokyo, Kokusai Bunka Shinkokai, 1938)
JAS	*Journal of the Asiatic Society,* Calcutta
JBRS	*Journal of the Burma Research Society,* Rangoon
L	*Life Magazine,* U.S.A., June 27th, 1955
MB	Cunningham, A.: *Mahabodhi,* (Varanasi, Indological Book House, 1892)
PA	*A Preface to Angkor,* (Phnon-Pen, National Tourist Office of Cambodia, 1960)
PC	Rajadhon, P.A.: *Phra Cedi,* (Bangkok, The National Culture Institute, 1955)
PGP	Lu Pe Win: *Pictorial Guide to Pagan,* (Calcutta, Sree Sarawaty Press, 1955)
RMTS	Buribhand and Griswold: *The Royal Monasteries and their Significance,* (Bangkok, The Fine Arts Dept., 1957)
SA	Godakumbura: *Sinhalese Architecture,* (Colombo, Dept. of Cultural Affairs, 1963)
SE	Wheeler, Mortimer: *Splendours of the East,* (London, Weidenfeld Nicolson Ltd., 1965)
SS	Sujata Soni
TCM	Hasan, Yakub: *Temples, Churches and Mosques,* (Madras, G.A. Natesan & Co., 1926)
VP 2504	*Visakha Puja B.E. 2504,* (The Buddhist Association of Thailand)

VP 2505-6	*Visakha Puja B.E. 2505-6*, (The Buddhist Association of Thailand)
VS	*Visak Sirisara*, Ceylon
WB	*World Buddhism*, Ceylon
YE	*The Young East*, (Tokyo, Japanese Buddhist Quarterly, 1964)
YTB	*The Year of the Buddha*, (United States Information Service, 1956)

Preface

Ever since I entered my teens I have been hearing much of Pagan, first from my teachers in school and then from distinguished foreign visitors discussing on Pagan with my father Dr. R.L. Soni, who has been quite interested in the ancient history of Burma. Later on, on reading his writings, any reference to Pagan made me feel very eager to some day visit the ancient capital which had been one of the most renowned in south-east Asia in the Middle Ages. The sentence describing Pagan as:

> the flourishing capital of a great kingdom, the seat of culture and civilization and the centre of intellectual and spiritual endeavours,[1]

remained stuck in my mind, making me all the more anxious not to miss any opportunity of visiting the place which had the honour of being the first all-Burma capital. On reading of art and architecture of Pagan by Professor Than Tun[2] and going through the *Guide to Pagan*[3], my interest in Pagan was further stimulated. At long last, the looked-for opportunity arrived when Professor Than Tun, head of the department of History in the Arts and Science University of Mandalay, decided for a visit of his M.A. Thesis students to Pagan and to have their reports on themes approved by him. Obviously, I was happy to be one of these students. Pagan is reached by river, road and air. Our group elected to travel by road on 25 March 1968.

The very first impression of Pagan was stimulating and charming. We found before our eyes a vast stretch studded over with numerous and diverse shrines or pagodas (Fig.1). It was verily a mighty unforgettable scene of history carrying our vision back to the great glory that was of Pagan from the 11th to 13th centuries A.D. Pagan, at one time a great and flourishing capital covering over thirty-two square miles along the eastern banks of the river Irrawaddy is pitiably in ruins since the 13th century A.D. It is today a mere township in Myingyan district of the Mandalay division (Map I).

1. Soni, R.L.: *A Cultural Study of the Burmese Era*, (Mandalay, World Institute of Buddhist Culture, 1955), 59.
2. ဒေါက်တာ သန်းထွန်း၊ *ခေတ်ဟောင်း မြန်မာရာဇဝင်*၊ (ရန်ကုန် မဟာဒဂုံ စာပေထုတ်ဝေရေး၊ ၁၉၆၄)၊ ၂၃၉-၇၁
3. Lu Pe Win: *Pictorial Guide to Pagan*, (Calcutta, Sree Sarawaty Press, 1955).

Map I of Burma Showing Location of Pagan in Mandalay Division

Note: The Division and States comprising the Union of Burma:

I	Mandalay Division	VII	Sagaing Division
II	Pegu Division	VIII	Kachin State
III	Tenasserim Division	IX	Shan State
IV	Irrawaddy Division	X	Kayah State
V	Arakan Division	XI	Karen State
VI	Magwe Division	XII	Chin State

Before we could carry our musings any further we found ourselves busy in settling down in the Government Middle School, our lodging place. Soon after dinner Professor Than Tun, notwithstanding the fatigue of the long journey, took the trouble of enlightening us with a long discourse on the history of the Burmese race going back to its proto-Burmese stage in the T'ao valley: it was a detailed and connected account of the various stages through which the race passed for 1000 years and more before the Burmese found themselves sufficiently settled in central Burma by the 9th century A.D. and later fully established as an all-Burma power by the 11th century A.D. under king *Aniruddha* with Pagan as the headquarters of the government.

Briefed by Professor Than Tun on the historical and architectural importance of the different edifices, we started our tour of the shrines the very next morning. In five days we covered no less than fifty-seven shrines, *Kū Bhurā:s* i.e., hollow temples as well as solid pagodas. Also, the museum housing the important findings from the place, was visited. The next four days were spent in visits to the shrines selected by different students for their special study. I on my part concentrated my attention on fourteen solid pagodas on which I submitted a detailed illustrated report on my return to the University. The commendations which it elicited encouraged me to persue the subject further.

A very look at the solid pagodas brought into vivid prominence certain architectural features which I decided to study carefully. My interest thus aroused got further advanced on discovering the evolutionary phases through which the *cetīs* passed in Burma. Moved and fascinated by this discovery, the decision was made to make the subject the theme of my thesis for the M.A. degree. Fortunately enough, this proposal of mine received an immediate approval by the head of History in the Arts and Science University, Mandalay, Professor Dr Than Tun.

There being no standard work exclusively devoted to the theme of my thesis, I had to approach various sources for the purpose. From March 1968 onwards I have been energetically engaged in the collection of these materials. Not only Pagan was visited but also the ancient ruins at Prome were seen first hand. While Professor Dr Than Tun's guidance at Pagan proved invaluable, meeting U Kyaing and visiting his Museum and Library at Prome and also the visit to the Government Museum at *Mhoaujā* were helpful. Moreover, U Bo Ke, the Archaeologist at Pagan, supplied some needed photographs and requisitely guided our photographer for some new ones. Besides meeting some Sayadaws (the Buddhist Monks) and visiting some monasteries in Mandalay and Sagaing, I spent some time at the Library of the Archaeological Survey of Burma, Rangoon, at the courtesy of U Aung Thaw, the Director of the

Archaeological Survey. Though I visited other Libraries also in Rangoon and Mandalay and approached Information Departments of the various Embassies at Rangoon, very little of value could be had from these except from the Ceylonese Embassy. Above all, I had to repeatedly approach Professor Than Tun and request my father Dr R.L. Soni for advice and guidance who both helped me with books and advice ungrudgingly.

The purpose of this thesis is to trace the evolution of architecture relating to the solid Buddhist shrines in Burma, with special reference to the Pagan period i.e., from A.D. 1044 to 1287. This is a period of special import so far as the Burmese race is concerned, for it was at this time that the Burmese, already in the land, more or less from "about the middle of the first millennium A.D."[4] as observed by Tin Hla Thaw and in a major wave for some two centuries i.e., from 9th to 11th centuries, attained the overlordship of the place. Beginning with *Aniruddha* in 1044, the Pagan Empire reached its zenith under *Cañsū II* (Narapathisithu A.D. 1174-1211). As observed by Dr Than Tun:

> It extented from Ngachaunggyan (near Bhamo) in the north to Tavoy in the south or even as far south as? Cape Salang for some time and from the Salween River in the east to the Chin Hills in the west.[5]

On the basis of an inscription of A.D. 1196, Dr Than Tun observes:

> The Pagan monarchy held sway over an area which is roughly the same as modern Burma with the exception of Arakan in the west, the trans-Salween area in the east and the major portion of the modern Kachin state in the north.[6]

Also, it was at this time that the transitional period, during which Mon influences were considerably at work, linguistically, culturally, religiously and architecturally, as testified to by inscriptions and archaeological finds, finally gave way to the supremacy of the Burmese wishes. Thus, not only the Burmese language by then considerably evolved and enriched to a literary status, became the official language, but also the religious architecture began to assume forms with trends towards finalization uniquely Burmese. This change is witnessed not only in the hollow shrines but also in the solid pagodas. While the dark cave-like hollow pagodas of the early half of the dynasty gave way to temples with more light and sanitation, the solid shrines evidenced transformation towards a bell-shape besides adding dignity and beauty to the structures through the imposition of requisite ornamentations.

---

4. Tin Hla Thaw: *The Development of the Buddha Image in Burma* (M.A. Thesis, School of Oriental & African Studies, University of London, 1963), 17.
5. Than Tun: *History of Buddhism in Burma (Pagan Period)*, (Rangoon Peoples' Literature Publications, 1962), iv. Hereafter this work will be referred to as Than Tun: *History of Buddhism*.
6. Than Tun: *History of Buddhism*, 37.

The Pagan period is unique in the history of raising shrines, not only so far as Burma is concerned but also in the context of the human history the world over as a whole. As all the kings of the Dynasty (Table I) undertook or patronized this building activity, the soil of Pagan got crowded with solid as well as hollow pagodas and also with monastic establishments. Alas! most of these grand and magnificent structures are utterly lost or are in a state ruined or somewhat renovated. The place suffered much not only through the Mongol aggression in the 13th century but also at the destructive hands of man and the inimical ravages of wind and weather during the last seven centuries.

Pagan today is no longer a place of political importance: it is rather a place of wonder and awe—wonder to the tourists who marvel at the grandeur that Pagan was in the heyday of its glory, and of awe to the Buddhist devotees, who get gripped with the sense of *anicca* on finding the shrines deserted and the place in desolation, a place where at one time resided and moved about thousands of monks amidst beautiful buildings and charming landscape, reciting the sacred texts or delivering sermons from high seats in the melodious words of the Buddha or their translations in Burmese. Notwithstanding the desolation, disfigurement and destruction, there are, however, fortunately still not a few shrines giving a good account of themselves. Of the hollow shrines some are quite imposing (Table II), the *Ānanda* standing as a prince among them. Of the numerous solid shrines, fourteen attracted our special attention. These together with some more (Table III) became the object of our special study to illustrate the evolutionary phases in the architecture of stupas in Burma.

Table I

Aniruddha	?1044 —	?1077
Maṅ Lulaṅ	?1077 —	1084
Thiluiṅ Maṅ	1084 —	1113
Cañsū I	1113 —	?1163
Ī m Taw Syaṅ	?1163 —	1165
Interregnum	1165 —	1174
Cañsū II	1174 —	1211
Nātoṅmyā	1211 —	?1231
Narasiṅgha Uccanā	?1231 —	1235
Klacwā	1235 —	?1249
Uccanā	?1249 —	1256
Maṅ Yan	?1256	
Tarukpliy	1256 —	1287

Before we proceed further with our study, certain facts need be emphasized. These are, firstly, that before the Pagan Dynasty of *Aniruddha,* Buddhism was not unknown, secondly, that before the Pagan Dynasty, Buddhist monuments were not unknown in the country and thirdly, that before the Pagan Dynasty, Pagan itself was not unknown. Long before the Burmese race entered Burma in a major wave about the 9th century, Buddhism had flourished for centuries among the Pyus and the Mons in the country. Moreover, the Burmans themselves in their early career in the eleven settlements in the fertile Kyaukse zone, through their contact with these earlier races, had imbibed to an extent the elements of Buddhist culture.

Table II

Name	**Place**	**Figure**
Ānanda	Pagan	12, 15 & 16
Sabaññu	Pagan	56, 58 & 67
Kanto, pallaṅ	Pagan	32 & 34
Thīlui Maṅlui	Pagan	57 & 59
Rhwekūkrī:	Pagan	60
Mahābodhi	Pagan	19
Puthuiwsāmyā	Pagan	61 & 62
Kūprokṅay	*Mraṅ:kapā*	66
Dhammaraṁkrī:	*Mraṅ:kapā*	63
Bhurā:sum:chū	*Maṅ:nansū*	65
Caṁpra kū (East of U Pali Thein)	Pagan	53
Kū Bhurā: (West of Mī:maloṅkyoṅ:)	Pagan	54

Table III

Name	**Place**	**Figure**
Chapaṭa	*Ñoṅ-ū:*	23
Rhwecañ:khuṁ	*Ñoṅ-ū:*	26, 27, 29 & 30
Rhwechaṁtoau	Pagan	31 & 33
Maṅgalācetī	Pagan	45 & 47
Ṅakywaināton	Pagan	28
Bhū Bhurā:	Pagan	17 & 20
Pepaṅkhyon:	Pagan	43
Mraṅ:kapā	*Mraṅ:kapā*	46 & 49

Name	Place	Figure
Hnatat cetī	*Mraṅ:kapā*	68
Hnatat cetī	*Mraṅ:kapā*	73
Cetī (South of *Manuha*)	*Mraṅ:kapā*	52
Scrowells Pawdawmu (East of *Sabaññu)*	*Mraṅ:kapā*	51
Lokanandā	*Sīripaccayā*	21 & 25
Phaklip (East & West)	*Sīripaccayā*	39, 42, 40 & 41
Cim:ñakñīama	*Sīripaccayā*	22 & 24
Caccanā	*Sīripaccayā*	36 & 38
Hnatat cetī	*Sīripaccayā*	70
Hnatat cetī	*Sīripaccayā*	71
Hnatat cetī	*Sīripaccayā*	72
Cetī	*Maṅ:nansū*	44
Dhammarājika	*Pwasaw*	35 & 37

Also, as quoted by Dr. Than Tun, Sir John Marshall remarked:

> Buddhist buildings existed at Pagan before the reign of Anawrata and that the monarch was responsible not for the introduction but for the development of that religion in Upper Burma.[7]

Evidently, *Nakywaināton, Lokanandā* and specially *Bhū Bhurā*: are earlier structures.

> (Even) the Petlaik pagoda, which is generally attributed to *Aniruddha* revealed some mouldings of older structure beneath.[8]

And, the residual but imposing Buddhist monuments at Prome eloquently testify that magnificent Buddhist shrines graced Burma further south centuries before *Aniruddha* sat on the throne of Pagan (Figs. *5, 6, 8, 9 & 11*)

> Before Pagan became the centre of the Burmese Empire which King *Aniruddha* and his successors built, there were many other Burmese centres or settlements around Pagan which would have had an equal chance of becoming centres themselves as they were all under the rule of local chiefs who invariably enjoyed the title of *maṅ*—the King. Subsequently the *maṅ* of Pagan became *maṅkrī*:—the great King—and was recognized as the leader of all Burmans.[9]

That Pagan was not unknown before the advent of the *Aniruddha* Dynasty is testified to by the fact of it as 'Pukam' being mentioned in two Cham inscriptions, which "can be safely dated (as) anterior to A.D.

7. Than Tun: *History of Buddhism*, 1.
8. Than Tun: *History of Buddhism*, 1.
9. Than Tun: *History of Buddhism*, 37.

1050,"[10] emphasizes Dr Than Tun. In these inscriptions, Chinese, Khmer, Siamese and Paganese slaves are mentioned as dedicated to a goddess. On this, Dr Than Tun further observes:

> Border raids were frequent in those days and probably some Burmans were captured and taken away to Champa to become slaves there.[11]

While evidence based on inscriptions in connection with the existence of Pagan before the *Aniruddha* Dynasty is very limited, the *Mhannan Rājawaṁ* is quite eloquent on the building of Pagan in A.D. 849. On this Dr Than Tun observes:

> Pagan must have been founded after A.D. 832-5 but not as immediately as A.D. 849-50 nor as remote as the middle of the 11th century. It ought to be between the two.[12]

The present site of Pagan mentioned above, however, is the fourth and the last site. The first was at *Yunlwat Kywan:* some seven miles east of the Irrawaddy,

> (where were) established some villages which, lodging as they were the Pyu refugees (from *Śrī Kṣetra*), began to be called Pyu-grama or Pyu-gama (i.e., Pyu villages), later abbreviated into the name Pagan.[13]

This according to the chronicles was in A.D. 107.

There is however, a decided difference between the earlier Pagan and the Pagan of the *Aniruddha* Dynasty. While the earlier ones were mostly Pyu in population, the last Pagan together with the other ten settlements, had Burmans as its inhabitants. Pagan of *Aniruddha* Dynasty meant not only the first dominant Burmese kingdom in the land, but also a centre of Burmese imperial rule over the whole of Burma. It was under such auspices that developed and evolved architecture typically Burmese. The evolutionary phases through which this development passed are dealt with in this thesis, from its earliest beginnings in India through *Śrī Kṣetra* of the Pyus to the last days of the Pagan Dynasty. The evolution of the *cetī* architecture at Pagan, basically and ornamentally, is discovered to mark a positively Burmese contribution to the Buddhist art. This, however, attained to its final stage in due course as evidenced by the *Rhwedagum̀* at Rangoon.

That Pagan of the 11th-13th centuries was not alone in the building of shrines is evidenced by a contemporary look at the neighbouring countries. In the light of this study, it is made out that though Pagan stood unequalled in its building zeal, other countries as well raised fanes

10. Than Tun: *History of Buddhism*, 3.
11. Than Tun: *History of Buddhism*, 3.
12. Than Tun: *History of Buddhism*, 2
13. Soni, R.L.: *Burmese Era*, 41

AP II of Pagan and Environs Showing the location of Pagodas

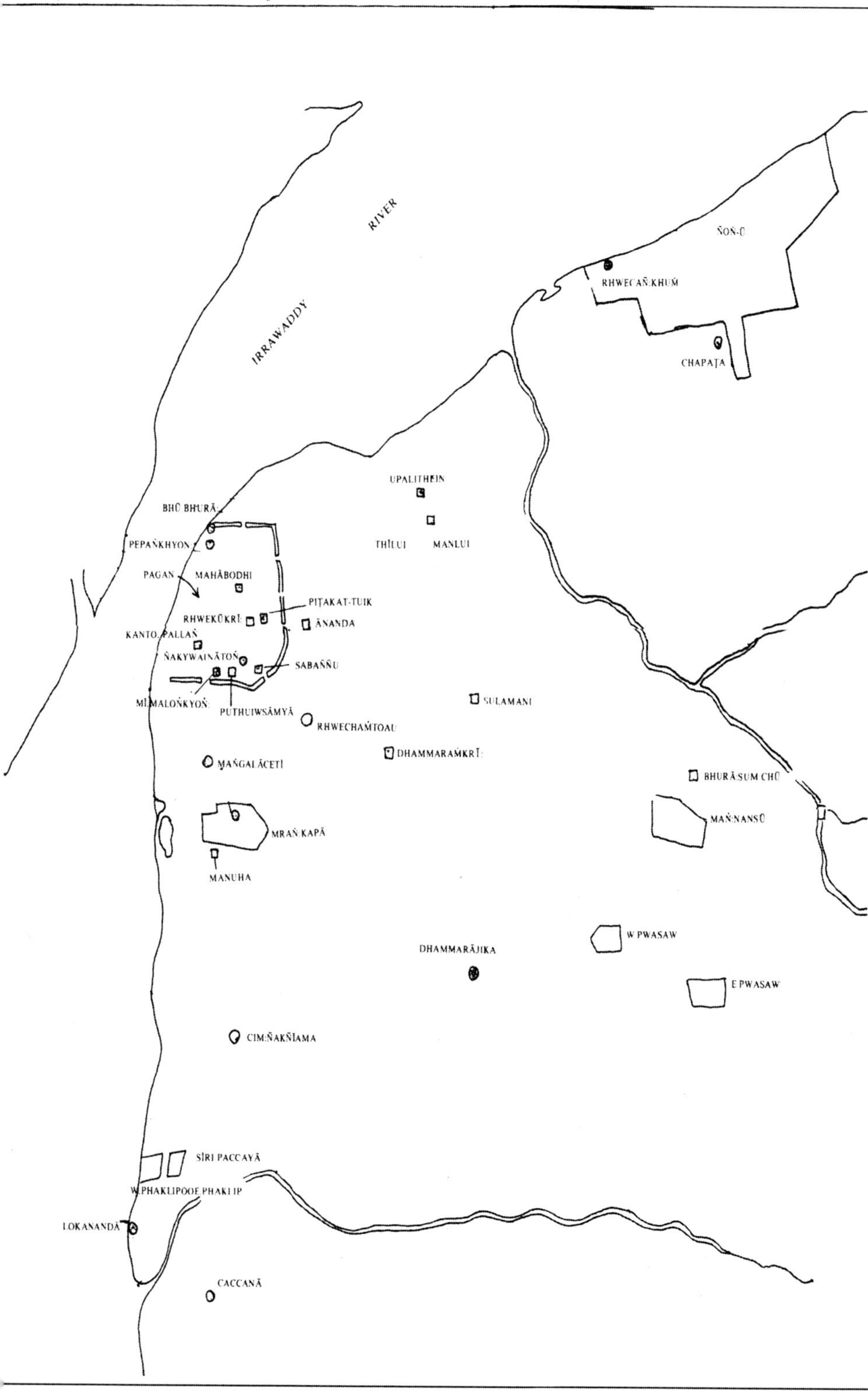

of exquisite beauty or gigantic proportions. A look at India and Ceylon to the west of Burma, at the Himalayan and trans-Himalayan regions unto Japan in the north, at Siam and Cambodia in the east and at Indonesia and other islands in the Pacific, confirms the view. Even as far as central America, structures are found giving the impression of being more or less copies of some Buddhist shrines in the east (Fig. *131*). This comparative study reveals the basic cultural unity of Asia, with the Buddhist aspirations as the guide line—a cultural unity which suffered a lamentable breakdown in the wake of the Industrial Revolution in Europe and the consequent partial or complete enslavement of most of the Asian lands. Now that a fresh epoch is in the making after the substantial liquidation of the European and American colonial and imperial grip on Asia, the resurgence of the cultural unity of Asia is once again becoming a matter of practical proposition. This inspiration is the natural outcome of a devoted study of the state of Asia contemporaneous with the Pagan Period in Burma. If effectively used, it can prove to be a great blessing for peace and stability in Asia.

With the lapse of time, certain illogical ideas have crept into the picture of the Pagan Period. Thus, the number of pagodas in ancient Pagan is stated to be fantastically high: this is endeavoured to be refuted. Also, certain ideas with respect to the shrines as memorials, monuments and mausoleums are briefly clarified, with a view to establish the exact status of the *cetī* in the Buddhist community. The causes and sentiments that made so many shrines rise on the soil of Pagan are also discussed in detail. A special contribution arising out of our research on the subject is the curious phenomenon of encasement of some stupas on the soil of Pagan with structures equally solid but not necessarily always of the same architectural design as of the original models. This feature is discussed at some length and certain plausible explanations are proffered, with door left open for further light on the subject through more archaeological efforts and historical research.

In fine, the evolutionary phases through which the *cetī* architecture passed through in Burma are uniquely monumental and Burmese. The result is a model wherein not only poise and beauty, harmony and charm, are visibly manifest, but also is witnessed the awakening impulse of spiritual dignity. It cannot be said what the future developments are likely to be. However, it can be safely envisaged that these shall be in keeping with the principles already at work. It is certain that the Burmese sense of elegance will not tolerate over-ornamentation as witnessed in some shrines in South India, nor will there be a return to the other extreme of over-simplification.

At the end of this work is appended an art section, which contains a large number of photographs. Most of these are reproduced from those procured from the Archaeological Survey, Burma, and also from published books. Of others, some are through the courtesy of U Bo Ke, the archaeologist at Pagan and others are our own. All these photographs, with the exception of a few, are of the Buddhist shrines in Burma and the neighbouring countries. A special section is devoted to describe all these photographs. Besides the photographs, some line drawings are added to illustrate certain points. In addition, there are a few tables and maps, which apart from detailing the kings of Pagan, and the names of the shrines, also help understand the geographical location of Pagan in Burma and in the context of the architectural developments in the neighbouring countries.

CHAPTER I

Philosophical Considerations

All along the length and breadth of Burma we find a great number of pagodas adorning the country: so much so, that Burma to the Westerners is known as the land of Golden Pagodas. Certainly, pagodas have been a special feature in Burma since the earliest days of her known history. However, nowhere else do we find the number of pagodas exceeding to that in Pagan.

Pagan, the ruined ancient capital of the Burmese kings, is certainly a living example of the unparalleled religious zeal the people of Pagan had for building pagodas. Even the residual number of some 5,000[1] fanes currently existing in Pagan from the days of her glory testify to this zeal: this is pitiably in contrast to some fifty shrines built in Mandalay, the last capital of the Burmese kings, during their rule for some three decades.

Pagan covers no less than thirty two square miles of area on the eastern banks of the river Irrawaddy. The vast ruins are spread out in what was known as "*Tattadesa*—the Parched Land"[2] by the Mons of the 11th century. Covered over with numerous edifices, almost exclusively religious, in various stages of decay and renovation, the place even today impresses the visitor of the grandeur that must have been of Pagan till the Mongol invasion in the close of the 13th century A.D.

A visit to the present-day Pagan, particularly for the first time, even though it be a mission connected with historical studies, cannot but give a philosophical touch to one's thoughts. A phenomenon as this is but a natural course particularly for one given to the observation of facts with an understanding heart. The interpretation of these facts in the light of the data at hand and the historical processes at work during the period under review is verily illuminating.

We have, of course, no desire to burden this treatise on a subject connected with history with questions of philosophy or with polemics lost in speculative thought. However, the fact is that there are certain situations wherein history and philosophy find themselves intimately associated and wherein the viewing of history and historical themes

1. Lu Pe Win: *Pictorial Guide to Pagan*, (Calcutta, Sree Sarawaty Press, 1955), 7.

2. Than Tun: *History of Buddhism*, 3.

through philosophical angle is expected to enlighten the understanding of the subject in hand in a way decidedly more comprehensive. Even though history and philosophy follow different courses and have objectives of their own, these do not, for the matter of that lack relationship with one another.

> Not only philosophy has its history but also history has a philosophy, which if duly grasped can not only lead to a correct appraisal of the contemporary events and of the material structures and ideological institutions coming from the past, but also provide requisite guidance for the channeling of history into the desired courses in the present and the future. It was the philosophical attitude as this that enabled Karl Marx to formulate his dialectical materialism, on the basis of which he laid the foundation of a new world order. This gave a fresh and constructive orientation to history in the socio-economic and political fields.[3]

In our approach to the evolution of the religious architecture in Pagan, we would do well to touch upon certain philosophical considerations. This, with a view to fruitfully widen our vision with regard to the limited material chosen as the object of our study. Abstruse philosophical theories or concepts being beyond the compass of this thesis, we are but obliged to limit ourselves to only certain philosophical observations bearing a direct and practical relationship to our study.

Before we get pinpointed to an intensive study of the few religious edifices, we feel instinctively reflecting on the situation. This, as a whole with respect to the ruined metropolis. The relevant philosophical issues that of themselves raise their heads are the following among others:

1. The stupendous vastness of the ruins,
2. The glory that was of Pagan in the days of yore,
3. The unlimited zeal of the people in favour of their religion,
4. The utter paucity of secular structures in the ruins, and
5. The international situation that occasioned the downfall of Pagan.

Out of these issues emerge certain questions. To the one with a religious bent, particularly with Buddhistic leanings, the very first thought will be that of the relentless operation of the truth of change or *anicca*. The city that was once crowded with life and activity and endowed with magnificence and splendour, perhaps unique in South-East Asia at the time stands today deserted and desolate.

> This law of *anicca* is incessantly in action throughout phenomenon, as much in evidence in things animate as in

3. Soni, R. L.: *Notes on History* (unpublished) f. 2 Hereafter this work will be referred to as Soni: *Notes*.

> materials lacking the vital impulse of life. The element of time is but a footrule to measure this ubiquitous phenomenon of flux and history is but a means to record the processes of change at work in the careers of nations, human institutions and ideological complexes.[4]

It was to this phenomenon of 'change' that Marx devoted particular attention. Going beyond mechanistic materialism and also beyond utopian or idealistic materialism, he advocated dialectical materialism as the proper choice for the coursing of the fact of 'change' towards progress in the historical sense. Men are not simply the products of circumstances, he said. Circumstances are changed precisely by men, he asserted.

> Men themselves are changed, not as a mechanical result of changed circumstances, but in the course of and as a result of their own activity in changing their circumstances.[5]

This is a lesson of vital value in the dynamic role man can play in history.

Even a casual look at Pagan, more or less dead for the last 700 years since the Mongol invasion in the close of the 13th century A.D. will convince anyone of the truth of *anicca* in historical events. While face to face with the terribly vast and very impressive ruins, one needs but accept that history is not only a record of inevitable changes but also a potent teacher of lessons for the future. Of course, one must learn to grasp the dynamic factors which are ever in operation in ushering in the change.

> Change there must be, if not for the better certainly for the worse. It is therefore wisdom to manipulate change in a way that history takes to courses progressive and not otherwise.[6]

Another issue of philosophical nature to be settled is the one connected with the terribly large number of pagodas in Pagan. The issue needs be faced that nowhere in the world, so far as our knowledge goes, the Buddhist shrines hailed as pagodas have been more numerous per square mile than at Pagan. Certainly, there are edifices such as the Borobudur in Indonesia (9th century A.D.) and the Angkor-Wat in Cambodia (12th century A.D.), which even in their ruins today are impressively extensive in dimensions and which must have been dazzlingly magnificent in the days of their glory. But, so far as the numerical strength is concerned, the soil of Pagan stands unbeaten in the number of pagodas it bore on its bosom. The obvious question is: why so many pagodas?

While the Christian communities even in large cities in the world, or major sections thereof, have no more than one church connected with each denomination and the Muslims and Hindus have only a few

4. Soni: *Notes*, f. 6.
5. Cornforth, Maurice: *Dialectical Materialism*, I, (Calcutta, National Book Agency, 1965), 53-4.
6. Soni: *Notes* f. 7.

mosques or temples respectively to cater to the religious needs of their followers, the Buddhists are found to have numerous shrines or pagodas in almost every city in the Buddhist lands. In Burma, with the exception of the villages which generally have only one or at the most two pagodas, the towns and cities are certainly found adorned with numerous Buddhist shrines. No matter who the builders, donors or supporters of these shrines be, all these fanes are open to public without distinction of creed or religion, race or nationality. The Buddhists in the building of pagodas are led by certain sentiments. Of these, four types merit special attention.

One of the sentiments is that to build a pagoda is an act of great religious merit to the person or persons concerned. The merit spells elevation to a better life in the hereafter or elevation to some heavenly abode or even unto *Nirvāna*. Of course, these persons at times may even declare sharing their merit with others. The sentiment for the earning of merit is quite strong with the Buddhists. This naturally inspires an average Buddhist to aspire to do his or her best to be able to build a shrine, if not in this life, at least in the hereafter. Obviously, there is spiritual satisfaction in doing this. Moreover, the building of a pagoda entitles the builder to be hailed as 'paya-dagagyi' or 'paya-dagamagyi' i.e., the 'honourable gentleman' or the 'honourable lady', the donor of the sacred shrine. This indeed is a coveted title, spelling not only spiritual satisfaction but also social distinction. Another sentiment is that the building of pagodas will enable others to use these for religious worship and for the practice of Buddhism which will help peace and happiness to prevail in the social context. Of course, the practice will raise the person ethically, mentally and spiritually (*Sīla, Samādhi and Paññā*), finally leading him to *Nirvāna*. Thirdly, the building of pagodas will help ensure the preservation and the perpetuation of the religion for long. And the fourth sentiment, though variably present, is the craving generally hidden behind the manifest religious zeal, for public applause and social gains. This though obviously not as laudable as the other three sentiments, is all the same with happy and demonstrable dividends in the personal field.

Sayadaw *Jeyapaṇḍita* categorizes the reasons under five headings namely (1) The religion to endure for long, (2) to gain merit for promotion to higher existences, (3) to be stimulated to walk on the noble path towards *Nirvāna*, (4) to create a spiritual atmosphere to save people from falling low or sinking towards hell and (5) to inspire the future generation in favour of high ideals.[7]

7. ဇေယျပဏ္ဍိတ (ညောင်ရမ်း ဆရာတော်)၊ စေတီဘုရား တည်ထားနည်းကျမ်း၊ (ရန်ကုန်၊ ၁၃၂၅)၊ ၃၀

Sentiments apart, there is another reason which occasioned the rise of numerous pagodas in Pagan. That is the surplus capital which the people enjoyed with Pagan rising to the dignity of an all-Burma capital for the first time in the history of the land. There being then no large-scale industrial and other such means to utilize the wealth, the people considered it the better of wisdom to invest it in the building of pagodas in their gratitude to the religion of the Buddha which had accomplished the miracle of uniting them into a homogeneous whole.

Sentiments as the above, among other reasons of national, communal and political nature, oblige people to build pagodas which go on multiplying from age to age and from generation to generation. While most of the shrines are built by kings to commemorate their success or to satisfy their religious whims, not a few are raised by the people to satisfy their personal religious aspirations. Some, of course, are decidedly with positive historical bearings on the national prestige. Thus, while the *Rhwedaguṁ* commemorates the Indo-Burmese religious ties, the *Kusuiltoau* at Mandalay and the *Kambha-e* at Rangoon remind us of the Fifth and Sixth Buddhist Synods of international Buddhist import. Besides, there are pagodas which are of historical significance because of these being the reminders of Burma's contact in the religious sphere in the past with countries such as India, the birthland of Buddhism, and Ceylon an important and zealous custodian of the teachings of the Buddha. (*Figs. 3, 4, 16, 19, 22, 23, 43 & 44*).

No less than 4,446,733 pagodas are mentioned as having adorned the ancient metropolis of Pagan. The same source mentions that there were no less than 4,346,733 residential quarters.[8]

> A seemingly preposterous numerology as the above has but to be accepted not so much as an extravagant stretching of whimsical imagination as but a frank act of poetic effusion. Ancient writings, Buddhist not excluded, abound in such descriptions. Strength of armies, extent of domains, population of cities, the magnitude of dowries, and the followings of great religious leaders, are all occasionally described without any regard for mathematical accuracy. Of course, these descriptions do not merit serious considerations: these only mean to be roundly accepted as simply signifying great numbers.[9]

In the light of the above we need have no objection to accept 4,446,733 the number of pagodas in Pagan—as the product of poetic effusion.

---

8. ဘုရားဖြူဆရာတော်၊ <u>သာသန ဗဟုဿုတပ္ပကာသနီ၊</u> (ရန်ကုန်၊ ၁၂၉၀)၊ ၆၇

9 Soni: *Notes* f. 8

Another question asked is: are these memorials, or monuments, or only mausoleums? Certainly, these are memorials in forms monumental or humble, mostly to preserve in eternal gratitude the memory of the founder of Buddhism, the Buddha, and in a few instances to commemorate some historical event besides. Most of these contain some or the other relic of the Buddha, or some personal effects of His, or His and His chief disciples' images, or some scriptures, along with golden or silver caskets inlaid or loaded with or surrounded by precious stones and other things of historical value. So far as the body relics are concerned, the pagodas might be labelled as mausoleums, but not mausoleums in the sense of being monumental sepulchres—which really speaking are vaults or tombs or buildings for the internment of the dead, the entire body or its cremated remains being generally buried there. Therefore, in the strict sense, the pagodas are not graves or tombs built over a major part of the body remains of the Buddha. Were this to be so, there would be only one or at the most two or three Buddhist pagodas in the whole world. That, however, is not the case. Obviously, the pagodas are shrines over a token relic or over a representation of the Buddha in images or his teachings, with a view to commemorate His memory and to worship the sacred elements to gain inspiration.

And, finally a word may be added. The solid pagoda in itself, as basically understood, is not without some philosophical considerations. These, however, will be discussed in due course.

Burma known as the land of golden pagodas is nowhere so rich in the number of pagodas as in Pagan. The very sight of Pagan conjures up certain issues, which oblige us to approach historical studies of the place with a philosophical touch. A pagoda itself even, architecturally speaking, is not without philosophical associations. The stupendous vastness of the ruins, moreover, reminds us of the glory of Pagan in its heyday, of the unlimited religious zeal of the people which made them bequeath numberless shrines to posterity and above all of the cruel hand of 'change' which spelt the transformation of the once magnificent metropolis into a wilderness which it is today. The causes and sentiments that made so many shrines rise on the soil of Pagan were, apart from providing spiritual satisfaction to the people concerned and giving them occasions to express their religious zeal for merit or gains through public applause, directed towards the use of the available surplus capital to enable others to practise religious life, thus helping the preservation of the religion for long. Also, it is explained that the pagodas are memorials in forms monumental but not mausoleums strictly speaking.

Chapter II

Evolutionary Phases

The soil of Pagan is crowded with pagodas hollow as well as solid, both types having a basic design of their own. The hollow pagodas architecturally are generally known by a central pillar where the relics are enshrined, with the four Buddhas[1] of the Kappa seated against it and looking outwards

> so that pilgrims coming to the shrine from four directions might find a semblance of the Lord who showed them the way to *nirvāna*.[2]

Around the central pillar with the images of the Buddha, is the corridor with porches on the outside and śikhara crowning the temple, thus giving to the square bottom a rounded and artistically moulded cover rising high in a beautifully tapering style skywards. The *Ānanda* stands verily a prince among the hollow pagodas at Pagan, the others being *Mahābodhi Kanto, pallań, Sabaññu, Thīlui Mańlui, Rhwekūkrī:, Puthuiwsāmyā, Dhammaraṁkrī: and Bhurā:sum:chū.* (Figs. *16, 19, 34, 58, 59, 60, 61, 63* & *65*). Regarding these hollow pagodas Professor Than Tun observes:

> **Hollow-pagodas...(seemed) to be more popular as they...(pro-**vided) four walls on which the scenes from the *Jātakas* could be painted as a decoration. Moreover, the paintings...(were) the most striking and effective means of convincing the common folk of the merit of giving alms.[3]

The paintings in the hollow pagodas, besides scenes from the *Jātakas*, also depict at places events of common or court life and alms-processions to the shrines.[4] We take leave of the hollow pagodas with this brief note and proceed on to study the solid pagodas in the light of the

---

1. At times instead of four there are images of the five Buddhas representing the Kappa as a whole..
2. Than Tun: "Religious Buildings in Burma, A. D. 1000-1300", *JBRS*, Rangoon, XLII, ii, Dec. 1959, 80. Hereafter, this work will be referred to as Than Tun: *Religious Buildings*.
3. Than Tun: *Religious Buildings* 80.
4. ရှေးဦး မြန်မာဝန်းချီ၊ (ရန်ကုန် ရှေးဟောင်းသုတေသနဌာန၊ ပြည်ထောင်စု ယဉ်ကျေးမှုဌာန၊ ၁၉၆၆)

evolutionary phases registered by them in the field of their architectural design.

Even a casual look at the solid pagodas of Pagan brings to one's notice two features with regard to their architectural design. These are:

1. that there is a basic structural design common to them all, and
2. that there are certain distinctive characteristics presented by each of them.

In other words, these pagodas, apart from following certain fundamental lines of architecture, are found to have a personality of their own. This is due to certain modifications in design and distinctive embellishments adorning the structures.

A study of the pagodas at Pagan is beset with certain difficulties, the most obvious of which is that the solid pagodas at Pagan are today not as they really were in their glory.

> It is not...enough to judge Pagan by what one sees of it today, (rightly observes Professor Luce and he significantly warns) one has continually to bear in mind what is no longer there. (He further adds): time has blunted or levelled every spire and pinnacle.[5]

Moreover, there were lovely details which suffered cruelly at the hands of time and weather, and recent 'merit-seekers' who wanted to simplify everything by a plain white lime-wash over old wall paintings. But, by far the worse damage has been through alien vandals mostly from Europe who "for decades past have souvenired among the ruins."[6] Besides the havoc wrought by time, inclemencies of weather and globe-trotters, there has been considerable change in dimensions and proportions in some cases through thoughtless repairs and renovations.

Nothwithstanding the difficulties involved in the study of the evolutionary phases in the absence of full-fledged original forms of the *cetīs,* it is not as difficult as supposed to visualize their structural evolution in the light of their available bare forms denuded of easily removable or perishable supplements and embellishments. This, because the original contour of the main body of the *cetī* is in most cases quite obvious. A study as this is positively assisted by the discovery at places of carved stone slabs on relic-chambers which show the original shape of their pagodas. A very important find in this connection was at *Śrī Kṣetra,* modern *Mhoaujā,* some five miles south-east of Prome in 1926-7 from what is known as the *Khaṅbhakun:* Two such carved stone slabs are shown in figs. 3 & 4.

5. Luce, G. H.: "*Pagan Architecture, A General Survey*", *GM*, Rangoon, I, iii, March 54, 25-6. Hereafter this work will be referred to as Luce: "*Pagan Architecture*".
6. Luce: "*Pagan Architecture*", 25.

A study of the contours of the main body of the *cetīs* reveals certain changes in design from age to age. As such, it will be of interest to pursue the evolutionary phases through which the pagoda architecture in Burma passed. A study as the above makes us look back not only into the history of Pagan architecture, but also obliges us to go beyond the Pagan Period retrospectively to the earliest known shrines in Burma at *Śrī Kṣetra* and thence to the earlier models in India which initiated the art of pagoda building in history.

Before Pagan came into prominence under the Burmese in the 11th century A.D., *Śrī Kṣetra* under the Pyus in the Prome zone in Lower Burma was the seat of Buddhist culture. Historical evidence in this matter is quite conclusive for, as observed by Professor Than Tun:

> Gold leaf manuscripts unearthed at or near the site of *Śrī Kṣetra* strongly suggest that the Pyu's knowledge of Buddhism was by no means slight.[7]

"The Pyus had occasional if not constant contact by sea with South India."[8] That the Indian influences were marked is shown by the old kingdom of *Śrī Kṣetra* being named after

> the sacred name of the famous pilgrimage city of Puri on the Bay of Bengal.[9]

This observation of Reginald Le May agrees with the findings of Dr. R.L. Soni.[10]

On reviewing the progressive modifications witnessed in the architectural field with respect to the construction of the solid Buddhist pagodas from the earliest times in India up to and after the fall of Pagan in Burma, an idea is had of the evolution the Buddhist architecture underwent. This period covers no less than some seventeen centuries. In order to understand the above said evolution, we would obviously do well to study the architectural situation in India, from the stage of the funeral mound, with which the history of a stupa begins.

The stupa, which now, architecturally speaking, is accepted as the basic structure of a solid pagoda, had, really speaking, no religious significance in its early career, which as remarked by Gokhale: "evidently goes much further into antiquity than Buddhism itself."[11] Quoting Block on the finds from the Vedic burial mounds, he further adds:

> According to vedic tradition the disposal of the dead in ancient India was divided in four separate acts, viz.,(1) cremation, (2)

7. Than Tun: "*Religion in Burma*", *JBRS*, XLII, ii, Dec. 59, 48.
8. Lu Pe Win: "*Some Aspects of Burmese Culture*", *JBRS*, XLI, i & ii, Dec. 1958, 20. Hereafter this work will be referred to as Lu Pe Win: "Burmese Culture".
9. Le May, Reginald: "*The Cultural Background of Burma*", *GM*, XI, ii, Feb. 1964, 33.
10. Soni, R.L.: "*Theri Khettaya—I & II,*" *BRMNT*, April 2nd & 9th, 1951.
11. Gokhale, B.G.: *Buddhism & Asoka*, (Bombay, Padma Publications Ltd., 1948), 243. Hereafter this work will be referred to as Gokhale: *Buddhism & Asoka*.

> collecting the bones of the cremated person and depositing them in an urn, (3) expiation, and (4) erection of the funeral monument[12]

That such monuments or mounds were in fashion at the time, is supported by Sarkar who observes:

> The Vedic literature, the *Śatapatha Brāhmaṇa*, distinguishes two types of burial mounds... viz., rectangular and circular.[13]

And, he adds:

> Also, the *Jātakas* refer to the building of stupas on the remains of deceased persons, and probably these were earthen mounds.[14]

For example the *Sujāta Jātaka*[15] *(Jātaka* No. 352) dealing with the life of Gautama as a Bodhisatta in the bygone ages mentions of the erection of an earth-mound' on the bones from the place of cremation of the Bodhisatta's grandfather. That it was customary to erect such mounds over the funeral remains is evidenced by what the Buddha spoke to his favourite disciple *Ānanda* on persons worthy of a cairn or stupa and also regarding the disposal of his own body-remains after *Parinibbāna.*[16]

> (Obviously), the Buddhists adopted the practice of raising stupas, following a custom already in vogue.[17]

rightly remarks Sarkar. This is supported by the facts that the relics of the Ven. *Sāriputta* and the Ven. *Mahā Moggallāna,* the topmost disciples of the Buddha, who died during His lifetime, were enshrined in stupas on His instructions.[18]

In due course umbrella came to be used on the top of the stupa in the case of persons of royalty and later even in the case of religious teachers. As observed by Harvell:

> The royal umbrella... was in the first instance a recognition of the social ranks, real or assumed, of the spiritual teachers whose ashes were deposited there.[19]

However, in the hands of the Buddhists,

> the social values in raising a tumulus were transformed into religious values and later on the stupa became a place of worship.[20]

While the stupa basically and from the architectural viewpoint is

---

12. Gokhale : ***Buddhism & Asoka***, 243.
13. Sarkar, H.: ***Studies in Early Buddhist Architecture of India***, (Delhi, Munshiram Manoharlal, 1966), 3. Hereafter this work will be referred to as Sarkar: ***Early Buddhist Architecture***.
14. Sarkar: ***Early Buddhist Architecture***.
15. Cowell, E. B.: ***The Jataka***, III, (London, Luzac & Co., 1957), 103.
16. Rhys Davids, T. W.: ***Dialogues of the Buddha*** (London, Oxford University Press, 1910), 156.
17. Sarkar: ***Early Buddhist Architecture***, 3.
18. Nyanaponika Thera : ***The Life of Sāriputta***, (Kandy, Buddhist Publication Society, 1966), 84.
19. Gokhale : ***Buddhism & Asoka***, 243.
20. Gokhale : ***Buddhism & Asoka***, 243.

definitely traceable to the influences flowing from the tumuli of the earlier ages, it was no longer a matter of mere sepulchre with the Buddhists. Even in the matter of location there was definite difference.

> (While the earlier sepulchres) were always built on secluded spots...(the Buddhist stupa) was built in a prominent place.[21]

As remarked by Barua, quoted by Gokhale, the stupa with the Buddhists "served as a funeral relicry and also as a memorial edifice."[22] Moreover, it while keeping the memory of the Great teacher alive, also helped to unite the Buddhists as a community, the members of which started paying homage to the Master. And, thus it was that the stupa became a place of worship.

Stupa worship marks a significant event in the history of not only Buddhism, but also of mankind. The interesting point is, as pointed out by Rhys Davids:

> that the only monuments of the kind yet discovered were built out of reverence, not for kings or chiefs or warriors, or politicians or wealthy benefactors, but precisely for such thinkers, who propounded fresh solutions of the problems of life. [23]

It shows the sense of proportion exhibited by the people.

It may also be mentioned that the worship to begin with was symbolic, it being directed to the relics or to certain elements in memory of the Master, such as a Wheel, a Tree, Footprint or even an empty throne. In due course the Buddha began to be worshipped in His image. This at first invaded the niches in the stupa and later became the presiding glory of the hollow temple as a whole.

The above observations clearly show the main stages through which the stupa passed in its evolution in India. These are:

1. Stupa as a funeral monument since the pre-Buddhist days going back to the Vedic age,
2. Stupa as a monument commemorating the memory of the Buddha and as such a vital centre for the Buddhist community as a whole, and
3. Stupa as a place of worship.

Evolutionary changes in the functional sense as detailed above were not without evolutionary changes in the architectural sphere. In this connection Mulk Raj Anand observes:

> All (the) elements of the stupa underwent gradual alterations in the several great monuments that grew up in India... For instance, the umbrella, the emblem of sovereignty which had

21. Gokhale : *Buddhism & Asoka*, 244.
22. Gokhale : *Buddhism & Asoka*, 244.
23. Rhys Davids: *Buddhist India*, (Calcutta, Susil Gupta, 1950), 53.

> signified the reign of Dharma, assumed many folds and began to look elongated... lengthening out into the form of a spire, so that the stupa itself began to look like a tower.[24]

Thus it was that a mere tumulus or a pre-historic burial mound got adorned with several umbrellas at the top. For example, Takht-I-Bahai stupa, and model of a stupa found in the tope at Sultanpur represent as many as six umbrellas one over the other, while a model stupa found at Manikyala tope has four such umbrellas. (Figs. *82, 83 & 85*). And, "in Bihar numerous models are found with seven"[25] umbrellas. Also, for purposes of religious worship we find how the stupa got vested with two perambulatory paths running around the stupa as in the stupas at Sanchi—150 B.C. and Amaravati—c. 3rd century A.D. (Figs. *76 & 80*).

With the stupa worship becoming a distinctive part of Buddhist life, further evolution in the stupa architecture took place. Apart from the elaborate gateways, steps, double perambulatory paths, crowning supplements at the top and other innovations on the body of the stupa, the intrinsic architecture of the very body of the stupa underwent certain evolutionary phases. For example, in Gandhara, i.e., north-western India, the original shape of the stupa was hemispherical.

> But the tendency of the Gandharan builders was... the creation of a structure of more height, which they obtained by elevating the stupa on a tall platform, and by elongating the body of the stupa upwards.[26]

This is evidenced in the model of a stupa at Manikyala tope ascribed to the beginning of the Christian Era (Fig. *85*). Also, in South India though the Bhattiprolu stupa, probably one of the earliest to be built, was a low hemispherical mound,

> in subsequent examples the dome was raised..., to comply with the natural demand for something loftier and of a more commanding aspect.[27]

This is exemplified by the Amaravati stupa—c. 3rd century A.D. (Fig. *80*).

Not only out of doors but in the earliest caves, the stupa begins as a rounded hemisphere as in the Bhaja cave—c. 150 B.C. and ends up as an elongated object in the later caves. Examples of these are Nasik—c. 135 B.C., Bedsa—120 B.C., Karle—1st century B.C. (Fig *79*), and Ajanta—1st century B.C. In this respect, Brown regarding the Ajanta stupa observes:

---

24. Anand, Mulk Raj: "Seven Lamps of Indian Architecture-II", *IM*, 2nd May 1948, 6.
25. Fergusson, James: *History of Indian & Eastern Architecture, II*, (Delhi, Munshiram Manoharlal, 1967), 152. Hereafter this work will be referred to as Fergusson: *History*.
26. Brown, Percy: *Indian Architecture (Buddhist & Hindu)*, (Bombay, Taraporevala Sons & Co. Ltd., 1942), 41. Hereafter this work will be referred to as Brown: *Architecture*.
27. Brown: *Architecture* 46.

> the stupa... is somewhat elaborated, its circular base being in two tiers, and the dome is rather more than a hemisphere, indicating a step towards that elongation of its elevation which characterized the later forms.[28]

In view of the fact that India and Burma were in frequent cultural and religious intercourse, the flow of influences in the sphere of art from India to Burma is to be accepted as a matter of fact.

> (However, though) the style of the Pagan temples and pagodas in its large and principal lines can ultimately be traced to... India,... it has characteristics, all its own, which entitle it to rank as a style apart.[29]

As regards the evolutionary phases in pagoda architecture in Burma, Professor Luce observes:

> Asoka's stupa—a squat hemisphere or dome of bricks—was lifted by the Pyu to cone and cylinder; contraction of the shoulders and spreading of the base is nature's way. It is as if the (people of Pagan)... saw and copied a Pyu ruin. But in the Pagan period the change was far from complete. Cylindrical and even bulbous forms persist. It was not till the latter half of the 15th century, with the Rangoon Shwe Dagon of Shin Saw-bu, that the Burmese *cetī* reached its present concave form.[30]

In between the final concave form reached by the solid pagodas in Burma and the earliest stupas constructed in India as exemplified by Asoka's Sanchi Tope, (Fig. *76*), several evolutionary changes in the architectural design are obvious. All the features of the present *cetī* show a marked deviation from the original design. The hemispherical mound in due course got raised into cylindrical and conical dimensions, as evidenced by the tall, imposing, cylindrical remains of the *Bobokrī:* and conical remains of the *Bhurā:mā* and the *Bhurā: krī:* at *Śrī Kṣetra* (Figs. *5, 8, 11*). These are at present one mass of brick from top to bottom. "Archaeologically they belong to the 5th century A.D."[31] Regarding the *Bobokrī:*, Professor Luce observes:

> the Bawbawgyi, which is the best preserved, is a cylinder of plastered brick, over 150 feet high, with a hollow shaft in the centre, crowned with a flattened cone.[32]

It seems there were other pagodas like the *Bobokrī:* type, for U Sein Mg

---

28. Brown: *Architecture* 29.
29. Lu Pe Win: *Pictorial Guide to Pagan,* (Calcutta, Sree Sarawaty Press, 1955), 8.
30. Luce: *"Pagan Architecture"*, 27.
31. Lu Pe Win: "*Burmese Culture,*" 23.
32. Luce, G. H.: "*The Ancient Pyu*", *BRSFAP*, II, 1960, 313. Hereafter this work will be referred to as Luce: *"Ancient Pyu"*.

U[33] quoting from report ASI (1909-10), mentioned of a small *cetī* represented on a marble slab very much resembling *Bobokrī:*. Moreover, he quoting U Mya says that on votive tablets, the representation of *Bobokrī:* are found.

It seems that apart from the cylindrical and conical forms, there were stupas with raised dome and the base also raised as evidenced by the two carved stone slabs on relic chambers in the *Khaṅbhakun: (Śrī Kṣetra)* (Figs. *3* & *4*). On this subject U Sein Mg U[34] observes that the design revealed on the two stone slabs shows both the stupas to be with an elongated dome and each with a ***harmika,*** i.e. a square box on the dome, but one has two and the other has five surmounting plates called '*Sattavali*' above the ***harmika.*** It may be mentioned that the expression *Sattavali* in its ingredients '*Satta*' and '*vali*' standing for '*chatta*' (sk. '***chattra***') and '*vali*', meaning 'parasol' and 'row' or 'string' or 'folds' respectively, signifies a row or string of parasols. Also, in the above design on the slabs there are five niches at the base of the dome each with a Buddha's image in *dhyānamudrā* pose. Obviously the *Khaṅbhakun:* contains the remains of one of the most ancient stupas so far known in Burma. It is interesting to note that the design of the dome on the two carved stone slabs accords with the design found at Amaravati—c. 3rd century A.D. (Fig. *80*) and also Mathura. For, as observed by Luce:

> Carved stone slabs found on relic-chambers (in the *Khaṅbhakun:)* shew the shapes of their pagodas, with umbrellas, banners and streamers, reminding one of Mathura.[35]

Reviewing the evolutionary phases undergone by the pagoda architecture, the following stages are discernible up to the end of the *Śrī Kṣetra* period.

1. The Sanchi stupa as representative of the original stupa (Fig. *76*),
2. The raised dome of the *Khaṅbhakun:* type (Figs. *3* & *4*),
3. The conical forms as exemplified by *Bhurā:mā* and *Bhurā:krī:* pagodas (Figs. *8* & *11*), and
4. The tall cylindrical form as shown by the *Bobokrī:* pagoda. (Fig. *5*).

---

33. ဦးစိန်မောင်ဦး၊ "သရေခေတ္တရာမြို့ဟောင်း"၊ ပသစ၊ အတွဲ ၃၊ အပိုင်း ၁၊ ဇန်နဝါရီ ၁၉၆၈၊ ၁၆၉
ဤကျမ်းကို နောင်အခါ ကိုးကားလျှင် စိန်မောင်ဦး၊ "သရေခေတ္တရာ"ဟု အတိုမှတ်အားဖြင့် ဖော်ပြပါမည်။
34. စိန်မောင်ဦး၊ "သရေခေတ္တရာ"၊ ၁၇၀
35. Luce: "*Ancient Pyu*", 313.

From *Śrī Kṣetra* onwards, the solid pagodas at Pagan took to an evolutionary course distinctively Burmese: While the BODY (Illustration A) ultimately became bell-shaped, the SATTAVALI (Illustration B) got transformed into the tapering spire with exquisite mouldings and other ornamentations like the two rows of lotus intercepted by beaded mouldings, surmounted by a plantain-bud-shaped finial, the whole structure being crowned with an umbrella.

Sanchi Tope
(India)

A Stone Relic-Chamber Cover
(Śrī Kṣetra)

Bhurā:krī: — Śrī Kṣetra

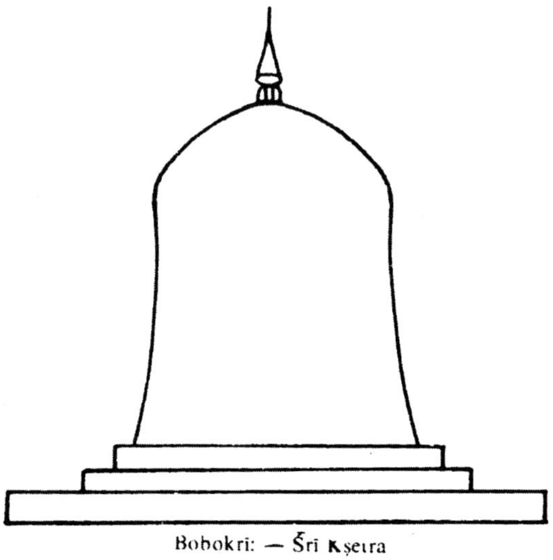

Bobokrī: — Śrī Kṣetra

Bhū Bhurā: (Pagan)

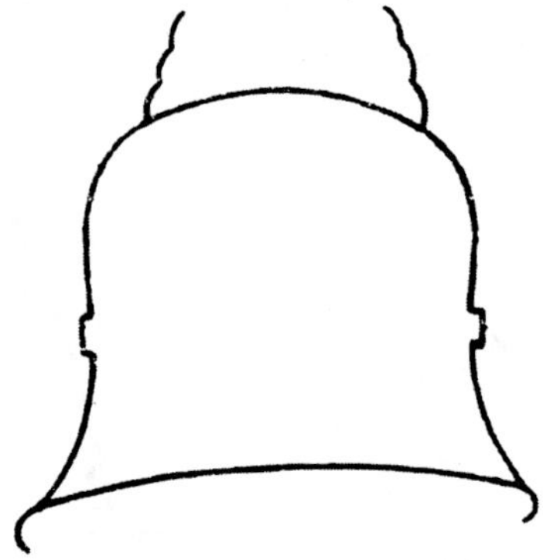

Lokanandā (Siripaccayā)

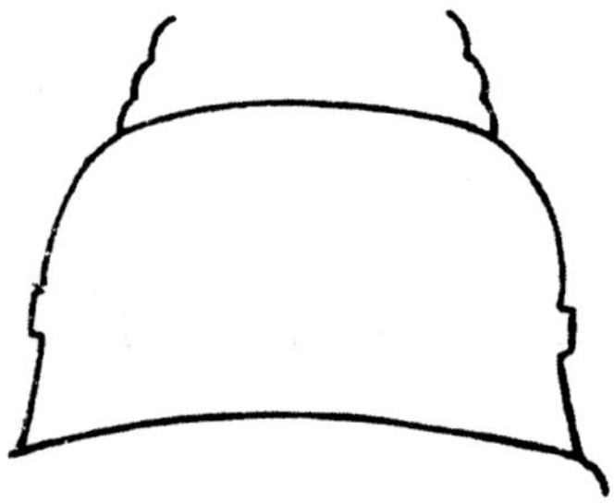

Rhwechaṁtoau (Pagan)

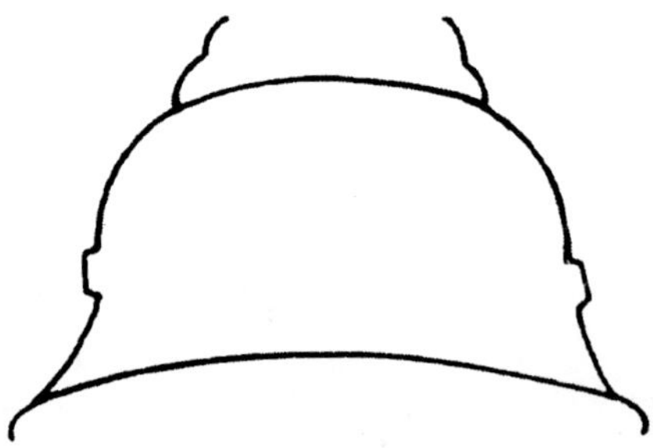

Rhwecañ:khuṁ (Ñoṅ-ū:)

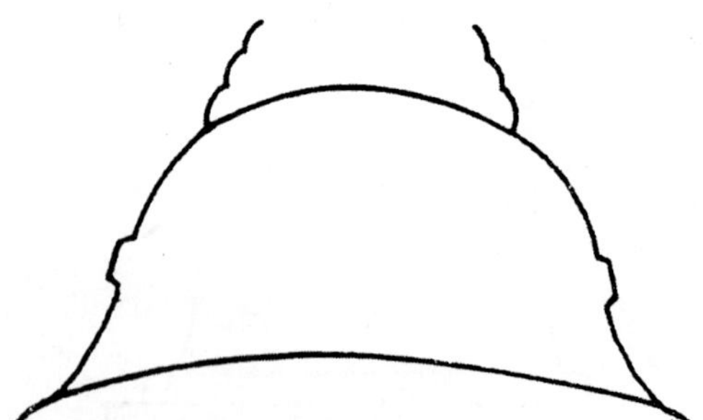

Rhwedaguṁ (Rangoon)

A. Sketches of *Cetīs* showing the body changes in the course of time

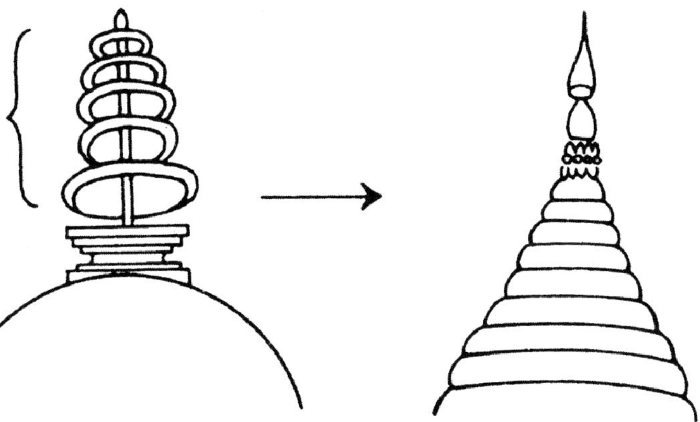

B. Architectural Evolution of Sattavali into Tapering Spire

Besides the body and the spire, even the TERRACES underwent architectural transformation at Pagan. (Illustration C). The three low terraces evidenced in the pagodas at *Śrī Kṣetra* got raised in the Pagan period as seen in the *Lokanandā* and *Cim:ñakñīama*. These in due course numbered five as at *Rhwechaṁtoau*. But as this did not fit into the Burmese sense of proportion and beauty, a return to three is seen in the later examples, for example in *Rhwecañ:khuṁ* and *Maṅgalāceti*. In the early examples at *Śrī Kṣetra*, we find no steps leading to the upper terraces. This feature is met with only in the Pagan period, where we find in the centre of each face a flight of steps leading up. (Figs. *14, 21, 22, 31, 26,* & *45*).

The *Bhū, Ṅakywaināton, Mraṅ:kapā,* and the *Lokanandā cetīs* are vital links in the history of solid pagodas in Burma, between the architecture at *Śrī Kṣetra*, and that at Pagan. (Figs. *17, 28, 46* & *21*). All these four pagodas seem to have been inspired by the tall imposing

C. Bhurā:krī:

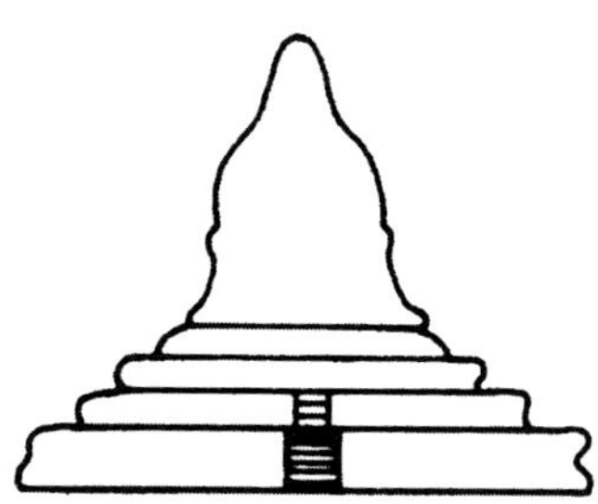

Lokanandā

C. Rhwechaṁtoau Rhwecañ:khuṁ

Bobokrī: at *Śrī Kṣetra,* their bodies being cylindrical in shape with slight modifications in each of them: In the *Bhū* and the *Ṅakywainātoṅ* pagodas for instance, the comparatively short cylinder curves in at the base whereas in the *Lokanandā* and the *Mraṅ:kapā,* it curves out.

The architectural evolution of the solid pagodas at Pagan, we would do well to classify on the basis of their structural situation at present. As such are offered three categories, namely:

1. Pagodas depicting shape of Early Period— Relic Casket Type,
2. Pagodas depicting shape of Middle Period— Mixed Type, and
3. Pagodas depicting shape of Later Period— Bell-shaped Type.

In the light of the above classification, the examples are as follows:

Early Period (Relic Casket Type)	**Middle Period (Mixed Type)**	**Later Period (Bell-shaped Type)**
1. *Ṅakywainātoṅ*	1. *Bhū*	1. *Rhwechaṁtoau*
	2. *Lokanandā*	2. *Rhwecañ:khuṁ*
	3. *Mraṅ:kapā*	3. *Maṅgalāceti*
(Fig. 28)	(Figs. 20, 25 & 46)	(Figs. 33, 26 & 45)

Bhū Bhurā:, however, calls for a comment: though in its present form together-with its spire, it obliges us to class it in the middle period structures, i.e., between the early and later architectural designs, in its basic bodily structure, it certainly is one of the earliest in Pagan. Among the later period structures, the *Rhwechaṁtoau* is early bell-shaped whereas *Rhwecañ:khuṁ* and *Maṅgalāceti* are full-fledged bell-shaped. The bell in *Rhwechaṁtoau* is convex but in the *Rhwecañ:khuṁ* which became the prototype of bell-shaped structures in Burma, it assumed a concave form. As remarked by Fergusson:

> In the older pagodas of Pagan the several mouldings (including the bell) are all more or less convex in outline, but in later examples,...(they have become concave); so far has that been carried out that it is sometimes possible to determine the date of

the structure by its attenuation.[36]

Apart from the above types covering purely Burmese forms, there are other types. Most important among these are what goes by the name of Singhalese types. Among these, above the bell-shaped body we find a square box-like structure. According to Fergusson:

> (this) square moulded plinth...by some authorities is thought to be symbolic of the chamber in the basement containing the Buddhist relics, and is in fact known as the "dhātugarbha" or relic-chamber... It forms an essential feature in all the Sinhalese Dagabas.[37]

Hence the name Singhalese Type. Of course, the typical Singhalese spire further adds to the distinction. Examples are:

Early Period	Middle Period	Later Period
1. *Pepaṅkhyoṅ:*	1. *Caccanā*	1. *Cim:ñakñīama*
2. *Chapaṭa*	2. *East Phaklip*	
3. *Cetī* at *Maṅ:nansū*	3. *West Phaklip*	

The *Pepaṅkhyoṅ:* the *Chapaṭa* and the pagoda at *Maṅ:nansū* village are classed as of the early period. (Figs. *43, 23* & *44*). On the other hand, the *Cim:ñakñīama,* a full-fledged bell, entitles it to be put in the Later Period. (Fig. *24*). In between is *Caccanā,* which is a model representing the Middle Period. (Fig. *36*). Here a passing reference to the East and the West *Phaklip* pagodas is also indicated. Whereas their high bottoms are indicative of the Later Period, their bodies conform to the earlier period structures. Hence it obliges us to consider these as *cetīs* in the Transitional Stage, i.e., the Middle Period. (Figs. *39, 40, 41* & *42*).

There is still another type and that is the Special Type or the Pentagonal-base Type. The *Dhammarājika* is an example of this type, its three terraces being pentagonal. From the evolutionary point of view this comes under the Later Period structures. (Fig. *35*).

This, in brief, is the sketch of the evolution in the architectural field with respect to the solid pagodas. It is really interesting to find how the Sanchi mound in India in the course of time changed in its form into bell-shaped pagodas in Burma. As aptly remarked by Fergusson:

> (the shrines change) from the solid hemispherical mound to the attenuated spire... till they lose all but a traditional resemblance to the buildings from which they originally sprang.[38]

The study of the architectural evolution of the solid pagodas, with special reference to the Pagan Period in Burma, covers a vast range of

36. Fergusson: *History II,* 343-4.
37. Fergusson: *History II,* 344.
38. Fergusson: *History II,* 347.

time. This study obliges us to go back into remote antiquity to trace back the beginnings of the stupa architecture in India. The architectural evolution had but to respond to the call of the functional evolution through which a stupa passed, the progressive stages in this sphere being stupa as a burial mound, stupa as a monument and stupa as a place of worship. With beginnings as these in India, the stupa reached *Śrī Kṣetra* in forms not only cylindrical (the *Bobokrī:*) and conical (the *Bhurā:krī:* and the *Bhurā:mā cetīs*) but also as slightly elongated dome—*Khaṅbhakun:* Type. However, it was at Pagan that the solid pagoda took to developments significantly Burmese, assuming bell-shaped form, as in the *Rhwecañ:khuṁ* which became the prototype of bell-shaped structures in Burma in the centuries that followed, with the *Rhwedaguṁ cetī* at Rangoon marking the end-point of the process.

CHAPTER III

Architectural Style and Decoration

Architecture is concerned with the building of an edifice. It is an art and science in one: art because of the style and ornamentations involved and science because of the design and the associated planning and calculations coming into the picture. Each structure, no matter small or large, unimposing or impressive, poorly built or magnificently raised, plainly designed or elaborately conceived, is the result of a detailed plan for a desired end.

Not only is "architecture... one of the most prominent of the fine arts"[1] but also is, as emphasized by Watterson, "the most universal of all the arts (it being) the one art which touches everybody."[2] Certainly, architecture, an intensively human art, is expressive of its time.

> An intelligent understanding of the history of architecture is a key to an intelligent understanding of history... Architecture is a part of the stream of history, history in stone. Every building in the past was built for a purpose which was meaningful in its time, by methods which were the most advanced for its time, and decorated in a manner which was the logical outgrowth of the culture of its time.[3]

Architecture, obviously, is an objective manifestation of the subjective designs in the minds of men, for, every edifice, notwithstanding its grandeur or simplicity, is but a projection in the world without of the plans conceived in the world within. The coming into actual existence of the edifice concerned is, as such, but a matter of the actualization of the dream in the mind of the architect and to an extent in the mind of the person or the group behind him. In this way architecture comes to have a definite ethnographic value, as supported by the observations of Fergusson who said:

> Every different race of men had their own peculiar forms in using the production of this art, and their own mode of expressing their feelings or aspirations by its means. When properly studied, it

1. Fergusson: *History*, 4.
2. Watterson, J.: *Architecture Five Thousand Years of Building*, (New York, W.W. Norton & Co. Inc., 1950), 3. Hereafter this work will be referred to as Watterson: *Architecture*.
3. Watterson: *Architecture*, 3-4.

> consequently affords a means as important as language for discriminating between the different races of mankind[4]

Generally what is found is that architecture served as the handmaid of religious impulses, it being employed as one of the principle means of providing places of worship. As such, the ancient temples and *cetīs* came to be the silent reminders of the spiritual genius of their times.

A study of the residual structures both at ancient Prome and Pagan, reveals the religious aspect of architecture. For, on a look at ruined Pagan and even what remains of the ancient city of *Śrī Kṣetra* in Burma, one meets only the religious structures: no architecture of the common residential utility is met with there, not even the palaces for the royalty and houses for the people. While nothing beyond a few temples and some tombs are found at *Śrī Kṣetra,* Pagan stands unique in the numberless shrines still adorning its soil. This, certainly, must not lead us to the erroneous conclusion that the ancient cities were exclusively religious in character, for there were in these certainly palaces and residential quarters as testified to by the Burmese and Chinese accounts. But the palaces and quarters, though grand and resplendent in magnificence, were built mostly of timber and other perishable materials, which deteriorated and got lost with the passage of time.

Indo-Buddhistic influences are obvious in the comparatively early examples of Burmese architecture.

> Yet all these structures, whether stupas or temples, while appearing to be fundamentally derived from Indian sources, disclose an attempt to effect in their design something original and indigenous.[5]

This makes the ancient city of Pagan the treasure house of Buddhist art and architecture. And this truly in the Burmese sense. These temples and *cetīs* were built at a time when Buddhism was uppermost in the minds of the people. As such it found expression in architecture of a grand order.

Etymologically speaking, the term Chaitya (Sanskrit), Cetīya (Pali), pronounced *Cetī* in Burmese derived from the term 'Cita' meaning 'a funeral pyre' has relics of the Buddha. The expression *dhātu-gabbha* or dāgaba is applied to a Tope as this. It seems certain that the sacred mounds at Nalanda (India) bore the name of Dagop in 1872 as stated by Henry Yule and A.C. Burnell.[6]

> (This is they add), the only surviving example of the native use of this term on the continent of India, so far as we know.[7]

---

4. Fergusson : *History*, 3.
5. Brown : *Architecture*, 208.
6. Yule, H. & Burnell, A. C. : *Hobson-Jobson*, (Delhi, Munshiram Manoharlal, 1968), 291. Hereafter this work will be known as Yule : *Hobson-Jobson*.
7. Yule: *Hobson-Jobson*, 291.

They add that the term pagoda is a transposition of the term dagaba, (which) is a genuine word, used in Ceylon, but known in continental India since the extinction of Buddhism only in the most rare and exceptional way.[8]

Not content with the term being a transposition of the term **dāgaba, they** have tried to see if the term pagoda could be a corruption of the Persian expression 'butkadah' meaning 'idol temple', or the Persian expression 'pout gheda' meaning 'a temple of false gods' or a derivation of the Portuguese word 'pagao' meaning a 'pagan', or a term connected with the epithet Bhagava used for the Buddha, or Bagavati, which got to be pronounced as 'pagodi' or 'pagode' These interpretations, seem to us to be nothing but a travesty of phonetics, as a matter of fact far-stretched interpretations of the term pagoda, which itself obviously is nothing but a hysteron-proteron or Hobson Jobson form of the word **Dāgaba**.

The solid pagoda has but one purpose, the purpose of serving as a repository of some elements sacred to the Buddhists. As originally this repository took the form of a mound, it was hailed a *thūpa* (Sk. Stūpa) meaning a mound. It is a matter of scriptural records that after the passing away of the Buddha the relics from His funeral pyre were enshrined in eight states in India. Each shrine was in the form of a mound and as such was termed *thūpa* or stūpa. Being places of veneration, worship was offered at these places. As such the stupa began to be hailed as Chaitya.

One of the oldest surviving stupas has been located at Piprawha on the frontier of Nepal and India. It is said to date from about 450 B.C. and... is made of brick.[9]

writes Mulk Raj Anand. He further states that the greatest example of early Buddhist art is the stupa of Sanchi (Fig. *76*) constructed on the orders of Emperor Asoka in the later half of the 3rd century B.C. And adds:

the stupa is a hemispherical dome, rising from a lofty terrace... The dome seemed to symbolise the sky... It (is) truncated at the top and mounted by an umbrella.[10]

As regards the construction material, brick is the commonest construction material found in ruined Pagan. However, in olden days says Luce:

the materials used were mostly wood, brick and stone. Apart from a few images and statues and some carved lattice-doors and lintels, there can be little wood-work at Pagan surviving from its

8. Yule: *Hobson-Jobson*, 653.
9. Anand, Mulk Raj: "*Seven Lamps of Indian Architecture-II*", *IM*, 2nd May 1948, 6. Hereafter this work will be referred to as Anand: "*Seven Lamps*".
10. Anand: "*Seven Lamps*," 6.

period as capital.[11]

Stone was, of course, used for diverse purposes but certainly far less extensively. It is obvious that the Burmese learnt the use of brick from India, for the brick monastery was hailed as the *Kulākyoṅ:*, which means a building put up in an Indian style.

The structure of a stupa, basically speaking, gives the vivid impression of architecturally symbolising the personal effects of the Buddha. This can easily be understood on visualising the situation with the robes of the Buddha duly folded and spread on a prepared ground, with the alms bowl placed inverted on these in the centre and over the alms bowl to be successively put the drinking cup and the walking staff or umbrella as illustrated below:

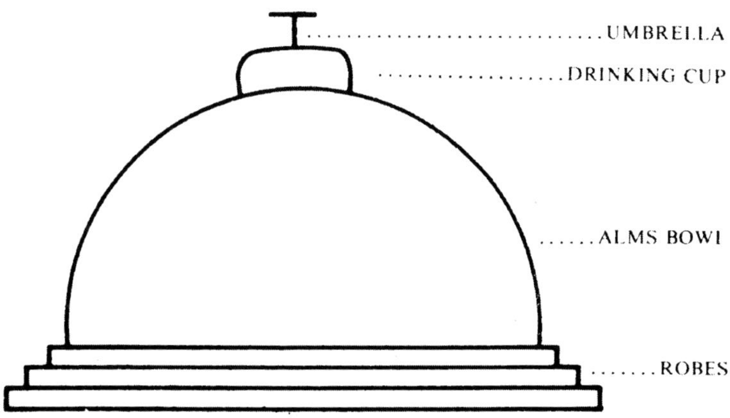

Coming to the parts of a solid pagoda, a typical solid pagoda in Burma at present has no less than fourteen parts. These are:

1. The Foundation,
2. The Base Platform which in Burmese is called *Phinaptoau* (the Slipper),
3. The First Terrace,
4. The Second Terrace,
5. The Third Terrace,
6. The Base for the Bell,
7. The Bell, representative of the hemispherical body of the ancient Stupa,
8. The cemented ringed spire telescopically tapering upwards,
9. Downward Turned Lotuses,

11. Luce: "*Pagan Architecture*", 26.

10. Balls,
11. Upward Turned Lotuses,
12. The Plantain Bud,
13. The Umbrella, and
14. Miniature models of *Cetīs* or *Kalasā* pots at the corners of the terraces.

However, to simplify the situation, a pagoda can essentially be divided into five parts. These are:

1. The Base,
2. The Three Receding Terraces,
3. The Bell,
4. The Cemented ringed spire tapering upwards, and
5. The Umbrella.

U Lu Pe Win observes:

> all these architectural features are purposive... there is hardly any architectural design or artistic motive in Burmese religious art which does not suggest any spiritual significance[12]

As remarked by Alec Robertson, the cardinal teachings of the Buddha are incorporated into the pagoda at every stage of its construction:

> The base stands for confidence (saddha)... the three (terraces) stand for the Buddha, Dhamma and the Sangha, the dome (or the bell) stands for the Dispensation of the Buddha-Sāsana, the tapering spirals eight in number stand for the Noble Eightfold Path and the Pinnacle or crown (umbrella) stands for Nibbāna, the glittering crown of the Buddha Dhamma. Hence, a (pagoda) is a living symbol of the All Enlightened One and his Dhamma.[13]

These, certainly, are learned explanations, which, however, might not be the exact interpretation of what was in the mind of the architect.

As regards the *kinds* of solid pagodas, there are four categories:

1. The *Dhātu Cetī* enshrining the relics of the Buddha,
2. The *Paribhoga Cetī* enshrining the sacred personal effects or their imitations,
3. The *Oddissa Cetī* enshrining images, and
4. The *Dhamma Cetī* enshrining the scriptures.

However, a *Cetī* is generally a mixed category, it generally having enshrined in it relics as well as images among other things.

> Each (*Cetī*) has,... a sealed-up chamber often in the basement and sometimes in the dhātugabbha which lies between the bell-shaped section and the finial.[14]

12. Aung Than Tun "Burmese Pagodas", *GM*, XI, x, Oct. 1964, 15.
13. Robertson, Alec "Full-Moon Poya Days", *WB*, XVI, ii, June 1968, 284-5.
14. Lu Pe Win: *Pictorial Guide to Pagan*, (Calcutta, Sree Sarawaty Press, 1955), 7.

An inscription dated A.D. 1227 at Pagan indicates a list of the enshrined objects in a *cetī* or solid pagoda. It is as follows:

> On Wednesday 22 December 1227, (the following)... (were) enshrined in the *cetiya*: the bodily relics of the Lord; the image of the Lord made from the branch of the sacred banyan tree; the image of the Lord cast in gold (and)... silver; the image of the Lord made of crystal;... ivory bezoar (and)... sandal-wood. (Underneath) all these relics and images are spread gold cushions and they are covered with gold umbrellas. Parched rice of gold (and)... silver, gold (and).. silver chandeliers are also offered. When these gems are enshrined, the (relic-chamber) is closed with bricks. After this, wonderful and magnificent figures of *deva* and various beings are made with stucco.[15]

A *cetī* it may be said in its present form is not a plain structure devoid of ornamentations or decorative mouldings. The decorative treatment of a *cetī* adds dignity to the shrine in diverse ways. The mouldings at the corners and the sides of the terraces and the presence of the *Jātaka* panels give a distinctive touch. Then there are the lotus-shaped adornments at the base of the bell besides the ornamentations applied to its body. Some *cetīs* have even beautifully executed niches in the body with figures of Buddhas facing the four cardinal points (for example the *Cim:ñakñīama cetī*) (Fig. *24*). Over and above the body is the ringed cemented spire: this has lovely embellishments in the way of lotus flower mouldings with ornamental balls in between. The entire thing is surmounted by a plantain-bud-shaped finial which is crowned with an artistic Hti. Additional decorative features are small *cetīs* and *Kalasā* pots at the corners of the terraces, which in some cases have flights of steps leading up. The remarkable thing is that the embellishments detailed above are executed decorously to give a touch of not only beauty but also harmony and serenity to the entire architecture of the *cetī*.

It would be worthwhile to review the situation with respect to the architectural style and decorations of the solid *cetīs*, taking representative examples of these structures. In doing this we will be limiting ourselves to the Pagan Period. Apart from providing examples of the purely Burmese architectural structures from the Early, Middle and Late Pagan Periods, thus emphasizing the evolution the *cetī* architecture underwent during this Period, we will deal with solid *cetīs* on the soil of Pagan depicting Singhalese influences and some special features. The *Nakywainātoṅ*, the *Lokanandā* and the *Rhwecañ:khuṁ cetīs* (Figs. *28, 21 & 26*), we have selected as representative examples of the Early, Middle, and Later Periods. So far as the Singhalese influences are concerned, we have in the *Pepaṅkhyoṅ:*, the *Caccanā,* and the

15. Than Tun: "Religious Buildings," 73.

Cim:ñakñīama cetīs excellent examples of the Early, Middle and Late Periods. (Figs. *43, 36* & *22*). The *Dhammarājika cetī* of the Late Period is taken as representative of the Special type. (Fig. *37*) While dealing with these a passing reference may also be made to other *cetīs* with a view to emphasize the comparative study of the structures.

A very look at the *Ṅakywainātoṅ cetī* (Fig. *28*) brings to one's notice the simplicity of its architectural design: even though it is beyond the range of conjecture to visualize as to what its top looked like at the time of its construction, the style and shape of the body and of its base and foundation, confirm the impression of it being an early structure, belonging to a time when the evolutionary phases in the *cetī* architecture had just gone a little beyond the orthodox stupa shape to somewhat an elongated dome. Moreover, the slight tapering down inwards of the body gives the suggestion that the structure was not a slavish reproduction of the earlier structures at *Śrī Kṣetra,* but a definite departure deviating in a direction remotely in favour of the bell-shape. This inclines us to accept it as a structure belonging to an early period—around the 10th century A.D Another feature worthy of note is the absence of any decorations at present around the body anywhere, except that there are some plain green-glazed tiles covering the body. Moreover, the base and the foundation were marked not only by the simplicity of structure but also by the peculiarity of their design, as a result of which there is asymmetrical configuration of the foundation, which, in the absence of any knowledge regarding the original name of this *cetī,* made the people name it the *Ṅakywainātoṅ* on the mere basis of its resemblance to the ear ornament known by that name. Just possible in the course of further research—architectural and historical—illuminating information may be had on the name, the contents and the original donor of the *cetī.*

The *Lokanandā cetī* evidently is, architecturally speaking, a representative of the transitional period (Fig. *25*). It is a decided improvement upon the *Ṅakywainātoṅ cetī* of the early period (Fig. *28*). The relic-casket shaped dome stands on a high base marked by three octagonal terraces, the lower two of which have steps leading up. Each terrace has not only beautiful mouldings and embellishments but also numerous plaques for *Jātaka* stories, as illustrated below:

The actual body is not only of an elongated dome of the relic-casket type, but also is curving out at the base, a feature which assumed a permanent place in the *cetī* architecture thenceforth. Moreover, the body, unlike that of the *Ṅakywainātoṅ cetī* is adorned with beautiful embellishments: these running as a rosette belt around the middle of the body are marked by crenated mouldings along the upper and lower margins of the band, which, besides has vertical floral mouldings of exquisite beauty double convex in shape at regular intervals, as illustrated below:

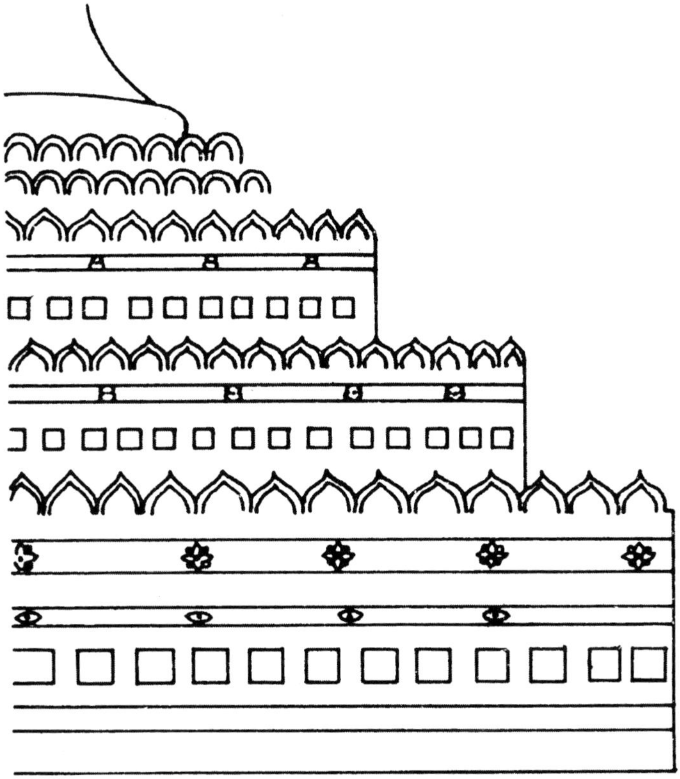

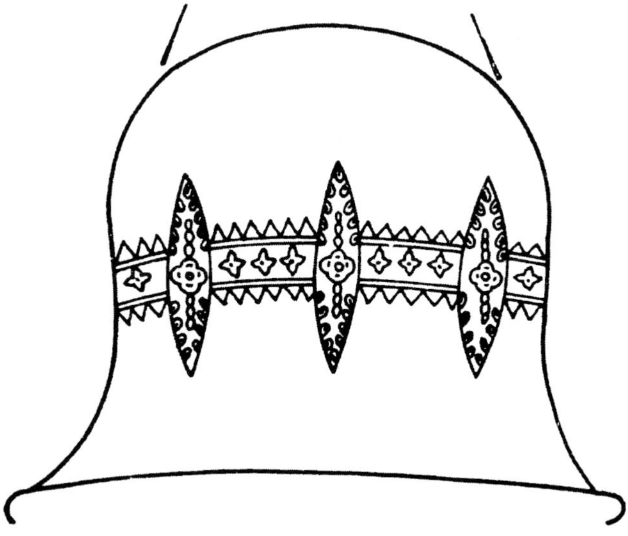

The dome is surmounted by a four-ringed cemented spire with ornamentations at its apex in the form of lotus and pearls which in turn is crowned with a plantain-bud-shaped finial, a distinctive feature of the Pagan Period: (fig. *21*). The Hti or umbrella above the finial is obviously a later addition. Even the adornments of the entire structure could possibly be considered as later additions. This however, does not rob the *cetī* of its status as belonging to the transitional period.

Another *cetī* categorized in the transitional stage group is the *Bhū Bhurā:*, this not because of its body which of the relic-casket type with its lower part slightly curving in is rather representative of a very early stage, but because of its spire which entitles it to be so classed (Fig. *17*). Fig. *48-c and d* taken synthetically come very near to the *Bhū Bhurā:* shape. The *Lokanandā cetī* (Fig. *21*) when compared with the *Bhū Bhurā*: and the *Mraṅ:kapā cetīs* (Fig. *17* & *46*) is certainly a further stage in the architectural evolution of the middle phase, as evidenced by the elaborately designed terraces, decorations on the body and mouldings of the spire.

The *Rhwecañ:khuṁ cetī* provides an excellent example of the finalization reached during the Pagan period in the evolution of the *cetī* architecture. (Fig. *26*). It is a full-fledged bell in form and the prototype of bell-shaped structures in the later periods in Burma. An 11th century structure, started by king *Aniruddha* and completed by King *Thiluiṅ Maṅ*, it is reputed to have in its basement the sacred relics procured by king *Aniruddha* from the ruined shrines at *Śrī Kṣetra*, and besides the frontal bone and tooth relic of the Buddha from Ceylon deposited in it just below the bell.

The *Rhwecañ:khuṁ cetī* when compared with the *Lokanandā* is a further improvement architecturally, even though its adornments may be later additions. The beautifully ornamented bell-shaped body rests on three square terraces having a flight of steps in the centre of each face. While the corners of the basement have lions with twin bodies, the corners of the terraces have *Kalasā* pots, the topmost besides having replica *cetīs*. (Figs. *26* & *27*). The terraces with floral edges are adorned with *Jātaka* plaques. A noteworthy feature of the design is that the sides of the terraces near the corner are thrown into four projections each (Fig. *30*) giving to the structure a singularly elegant look. Similar projections are witnessed in the *Maṅgalācetī* and the *Rhwechaṁtoau cetīs* (Figs. *47* & *33*). Here it may be mentioned that while the number of terraces in *Maṅgalācetī* is the same as in the *Rhwecañ:khuṁ cetī*, the number is raised to five in the *Rhwechaṁtoau cetī*. Also, it needs be added that the *Maṅgalācetī* has *Kalasā* pots and *cetī* replicas as in the *Rhwecañ:khuṁ cetī*. *Jātaka* plaques are witnessed also in the terraces of the *Maṅgalācetī*.

As regards the body which is frankly bell-shaped, it has noteworthy ornamentations. The bell has a central rosette band with toothing above and kirtimukha frieze below. (Figs. *27* & *29*). Also, just below the spire are floral mouldings running around. In contradistinction to these elaborate and multiple ornamentations on the bell of the *Rhwecañ:khuṁ,* the ornamentations at the *Rhwechaṁtoau* and the *Maṅgalāceti* are very much simplified, besides being limited to the belt around the bell (Figs. *31* & *45*).

The dome is surmounted by a cemented ringed spire telescopically tapering upwards. The top of it is ornamented with downturned and upturned lotuses with ball-shaped mouldings in between. Above it is a plantain-bud-shaped finial. The umbrella which is a later addition gives a finishing touch to the top. Mention needs be made that the spires of the *Rhwechaṁtoau* and the *Maṅgalācetī* have decorations more or less matching that of the *Rhwecañ:khuṁ cetī.*

A feature of distinction in connection with the *Rhwecañ:khuṁ cetī* is the depiction there of the thirty-seven nats. These figures are lodged in a corner of the platform. This distinguishes the *Rhwecañ:khuṁ cetī* from all other *cetīs* in Pagan. It also brings into prominence a vital feature in the history of the Theravāda in Burma. The feature is the transitional and compromising stage through which the country was passing from the religious beliefs characterized by nat worship to a frankly Theravāda belief.

Besides the representative specimens given above of architectural style and decorations connected with the *cetīs* in the Pagan period, there are certain architectural modifications met with during the same period, which must not miss our attention. Two of these merit special attention. The *Dhammarājika cetī* is a special architectural modification in the way that all its three terraces are pentagonal in shape. The bell-shaped dome having a central rosette band with toothing above and *kirtimukha* frieze below surmounted by a cemented ringed spire telescopically tapering upwards rests on three pentagonal terraces with replica *cetīs* at the corners of the third terrace. The terraces having steps are adorned with *Jātaka* plaques and there are image houses at the base on all the five sides. (Fig. *37*).

The second modification in the architectural structure of the Pagan *cetī* is the incorporation in their design of a feature commonly met with in the dagabas in Ceylon. This feature finds expression in the addition of a special structure on the top of the dome of the stupa. Generally in the shape of a square box it is at times a modified box in shape and even a circular curvilinear structure at other times. Though truly speaking not a Singhalese innovation in the sense that it was invented or first used in Ceylon, it having been in use in some cases in India in the early period of the Buddhist art (examples are the Sanchi and the Karle stupas

(Figs. *76* & *79*); all the same it came to be designated a Singhalese feature in the field of art because of its universal application to the dagabas in that country. A feature of note is that the structure mentioned above together with the spire above it, gives to a *cetī* the touch of Singhalese design. The spire unlike that of a Burmese *cetī* in the orthodox sense, is with certain features unique to itself, the features being that it has no umbrella at the top and at the bottom it is separated from the box by indentation differing in height in different *cetīs.* While in the *Cim:ñakñīama cetī* the indentation is insignificant, it is well marked in the *Pepaṅkhyoṅ:* and the *Chapaṭa cetīs* (Figs. *22, 43* & *23*). A noteworthy point brought to our notice is that the finials of the Singhalese spire and that of the Burmese during the Pagan Period, though not exactly alike are somewhat similar in shape, the one being more or less semi-circular and the other plantain-bud shaped. (Figs. *51, 52, 53* & *54*). In this connection, the right side of Fig. *50* ending in 'g' reminds us of the evolution of the Chatta and the Satti into a knobbed structure.

The two structures mentioned above taken together give to a *cetī* the name of Singhalese type. Such types are met with in the Pagan Period incorporated in the body of the *cetīs* of the Early, Middle as well as of the Late periods. An example of the early type is the *Pepaṅkhyoṅ: cetī.* While its elongated dome rests on a low foundation, the *Chapaṭa cetī* and the *cetī* at *Maṅ:nansū* village also representing the early evolutionary stages of the body of the *cetī*, are with high foundations which besides are very well ornamented. (Figs. *43, 23* & *44*). These two, obviously, represent a later phase in the history of the early type.

The *Caccanā cetī* is a good representative of the middle period. It is a decided improvement upon the *Pepaṅkhyoṅ: cetī* of the early period: herein not only the body is assuming the bell-shape but also there are terraces, four in number each with *Jātaka* plaques and having replica *cetī* at their corners. (Fig. *36*). As regards the *Phaklip cetī* which are more or less in a ruined state (Figs. *39* & *40*), they give the impression of belonging to the transitional stage, i.e., the Middle Period.

The *Cim:ñakñīama cetī* obviously is a model worthy to be categorized along with the later architectural developments. (Figs. *22* & *24*). It, obviously is a further improvement on the *Caccanā cetī*—architecturally as well as from the point of view of adornments. The richly ornamented bell-shaped body rests on three square terraces lacking any steps, and having replica *cetīs* at the corners of the first and third terraces and *kalasā* pots at the corners of the second terrace. The projections at the corners give to the structure an elegant appearance. The exquisitely carved body has a central rosette band, with toothing above and *kirtimukha* frieze below. In between are highly ornamented niches, each facing the cardinal points and having enshrined in it a small image of the Budhha. The bell-shaped dome is surmounted by a foliated box which in turn is crowned with a spire ending in a semi-circular top.

A noteworthy feature of the Singhalese Type *cetī* is the absence of steps. This is clearly seen in the *Caccanā* and the *Cim:ñakñīama cetīs*. Here it may also be mentioned that our categorization of the Singhalese *cetīs*, into Early, Middle and Late periods is mainly concerned with the architectural style: it in no way commits us with respect to the adornment, which may be later additions.

Architecture is an art and science in one. It is an objective manifestation of the culture of its times. Hence, it comes to have a definite ethnographic value. Architecture is generally found to serve as the handmaid of religious impulses. And, this is clearly discernible in Pagan. The buildings of Pagan may be most nearly defined as fundamentally of Indian extraction but designed and adopted to conform to Burmese conceptions. In Burma the solid shrine is hailed as *cetī* which obviously is an abbreviation of the Indian term Chaitya or place of worship. The English version is Pagoda which is a reversal of the Singhalese term Dāgaba (*Dhātu-gabbha*). The solid pagoda or *cetī* being a repository of some relics (i.e., *dhātu*) or other religious elements, is sacred to the Buddhists. As originally this repository took the form of a mound, it was hailed a stūpa. Being a place of veneration, worship was offered at the *cetī*. Each *cetī* has a sealed-up chamber often in the basement and sometimes in the dhātu-gabbha which lies between the bell and the finial. As regards the construction material, so far as a *cetī* is concerned, brick was the commonest material, stone being sparingly used. A pagoda can be divided into (1) the base, (2) the three receding terraces, (3) the bell, (4) the cemented ringed spire tapering upwards and (5) the umbrella. There are in terms of their contents four kinds of *cetīs* (1) The *Dhātu cetī*, (2) the *Paribhoga cetī*, (3) the *Oddissa cetī* and (4) the *Dhamma cetī*. However, a *cetī* is generally a mixed category. A survey of the Architectural Style of the *cetīs* at Pagan brings into view certain features distinctively unique. The most salient feature is the evolutionary phases which these *cetīs* underwent under the influence of the Burmese culture. This influence is found pervading in almost all the structural sections of their design. The terraces, the body and the spire assumed forms, which progressively evolved to a standard basic type. This type became the prototype of similar structures in the later periods. While the *Ṅakywaiṅātoṅ* represents the earliest model and the *Lokanandā* the transitional phase, the *Rhwecañ:khuṁ* is an excellent example of the fully evolved Pagan *cetī*. Each of these represents a distinctive architectural improvement upon the types representing the earlier structures: while the terraces changed in number from three to five and finally back to three, the body progressively tended towards a bell-shape, and the top in stages evolved to be a moulded spire of graceful beauty crowned with plantain-bud shaped finial which in later ages got further adorned with umbrella and diamond bud. Besides the architectural designs typically Burmese there also arose during the Pagan Period some *cetīs* with definitely alien features, the noteworthy among which being **those of the Singhalese innovation and the Pentagonal-base type** (*Dhammarājika*). Apart from the architectural evolution designated into Early, Middle and Late Periods of the Singhalese design as exemplified by the *Pepaṅkhyoṅ:*, the *Caccanā* and the *Cim:ñakññama* respectively, the feature of ornamentation showed itself. This in forms vivid and vivacious gave a touch of serene beauty and majestic impressiveness to the shrine as a whole. The noteworthy fact is that in spite of the basic form remaining discernible architecturally in all the *cetīs*, each one had a distinctive personality of its own in form as well as in ornamentations.

CHAPTER IV

Restoration and Encasement of Solid Pagodas

There are several pagodas or Buddhist shrines in Burma, particularly those of special historical value, that have undergone improvement through minor renovation or have been submitted to substantial restoration through requisite repairs : some have even been subjected to worthwhile extensions, from time to time, with even certain modern adnexa added, such as the lifts in the case of the *Rhwedagum̀* at Rangoon and the *Rhwecham̀toau* at Prome. The repairs and renovations are done despite the view commonly and currently held, peculiar to Burma, that a shrine once raised merited no more attention ıor its structural integrity. A view as this derives its strength from the meaningless superstitions that only the one who raised the fane was entitled to the spiritual gain accruing from its construction, that the merit was attained once the structure was raised and duly dedicated, and that once the ceremony of dedication was over, there was no more merit to be gained by attending to the structure if it subsequently needed any more repairs to sustain its structural integrity or appearance in general. That this superstitious view is mainly responsible for the attitude of neglect most of the solid as well as other shrines suffered, is well evidenced by the state of disrepair and subsequent crumbling witnessed in a large number of religious edifices all over Burma.

Notwithstanding what is said above on the subject of non-attention to the act of proper repairs of a shrine once dedicated, the fact is patent that some inscriptions of the Pagan Period testify to the donation by the patrons, of adequate means—productive lands, staff of personnel and even material assets—for the subsequent maintenance of the religious structures. As observed by Dr Than Tun:

> A donor... in A.D. 1198, dedicated to a pagoda 567 ½ pay of land and 228 slaves, the majority of whom were labourers who served the pagoda with the produce of the land, and the rest were slaves who were skilled artists. ... *Anàntasura* in A.D. 1223 clearly defined ... (the slaves) duties as follows: to go on forever doing the

necessary repairs (at the establishment); to sweep the compound;
to go on serving the Lord and the Law without intermission.[1]

This shows that the superstition referred to above most probably came into being in the later ages.

Fortunately enough, the superstition mentioned above is not shared by the governmental authorities in Burma, who consider it highly meritorious from the national and cultural points of view to preserve the ancient structures of proved historical value to enthuse and inspire the future generations in their national heritage. It is thus, that archaeology has not only unearthed valuable finds but also has endeavoured at considerable cost to preserve certain monumental items for posterity. As a matter of fact, the selected monuments are officially listed,[2] and considerable funds are set apart annually in the national budget for the purpose of conserving these.

Conservation and renovation of the selected historical monuments have become one of the important duties of the Cultural Ministry of the Government of Burma. While this work is proceeding apace in the district of Mandalay, the last seat of the Burmese Monarchy, the ancient shrines in Pagan and also in other parts of the country, are receiving quite an energetic attention. These activities of the authorities are mainly directed towards the regeneration and renovation of the ruined structures in a way that these come up to be as near the original form in shape, size and adornments as possible: examples are seen in the four *cetīs* at Pagan (Figs. *51, 52, 53* & *54*). As regards the *Bobokrī*: (Fig. *5*) at *Śrī Kṣetra*, while its body form is more or less maintained in its original shape, its top having been absent ever since archaeology started its work in Burma is with a new form. Certainly, some structures, for want of full information on their original form or for some other reason, suffer positive improvement in the modern sense, which however to an extent or even substantially robs them of their merited touch of antiquity. A confusion is thus likely to arise in the assessment of the historical antiquity of certain structures. Such a state of affairs can, however, be easily guarded against by putting up new inscriptions, detailing the nature and date of the renovation effected, in a way that the inscription is not only not easily lost, but also easily available for study.

Historical monuments—as a matter of fact, all edifices—need their architectural integrity to be maintained through periodic or timely requisite repairs. If this, for some reason or the other, is not done, the structures suffer breakdown in time and with continued neglect the process goes ahead till the structures crumble down and are either

1. Than Tun: "Social Life in Burma, A.D. 1044-1287", *JBRS*, XLI, i & ii, Dec. 1958, 44-6.
2. *Amended List of Ancient Monuments in Burma*, (Rangoon, Supdt., Government Printing and Staty., Union of Burma, 1960).

irretrievably lost and covered over with forests or their renovation spells the marshalling of huge funds, which are not easily available. This is what actually more or less happened to some of the deserted capitals in the east, noteworthy among which are Anuradhapura in Ceylon, the Borobudur at Java, the Ankors in Cambodia and, of course, Pagan in Burma. Fortunately enough, in contrast to the structure at Anuradhapura and the Ankors in Cambodia which got covered over with impenetrable forests through centuries, many of the shrines in Pagan and also the Borobudur at Java remained in a fairly good state of preservation, which made the process of renovation in most cases not as difficult as it otherwise would have been. However, recently the Borobudur has begun to defy ordinary acts of repair and is attracting worldwide attention for a study of the precarious situation connected with it, so that it may be saved from utter collapse as threatened by a part of it.

Regrettably enough in Pagan much harm has been found inflicted on some of the edifices through reckless attempts at repairs or through thoughtless acts of beautification by citizens of the place. Although the beautification was out of good intentions and pious impulses, it ruined the structures from the architectural point of view. Besides the changes brought in the shrines through requisite or irregular repairs and renovations, and the harm done by treasure hunters in Burma and curio-collectors from home and abroad, there is another change that needs attention. This, a phenomenon in itself, is marked by the encasement of the original shrine by solid and at times massive covers.

The feature of encasement is by no means a recent innovation, for it dates back to the earliest days of the solid shrines. It is testified to by the fact of history, a classical and very ancient example of it being the solid stupa at Sanchi (Fig. *76*). For, according to Sir John Marshall:

> the original *brick* stūpa built by Asoka was probably of not more than half the present dimensions, which were subsequently enlarged by the addition of a *stone* casing faced with concrete. ... A similar fate has possibly overtaken many other stupas of Asoka.[3]

The encasement of solid pagodas is found to be of three varieties:

1. Firstly, a solid encasement intimately covering the original structure,
2. Secondly, an encasement enveloping the original shrine with empty space in between, and
3. Thirdly, the encasement may be multiple, one covering fixed over another intimately adjoining with one another, without any space

3. Majumdar, Raychaudhuri & Datta: *An Advanced History of India*, (New York, St. Martin's Press, 1965), 228. Hereafter this work will be referred as Majumdar et. al: *History*.

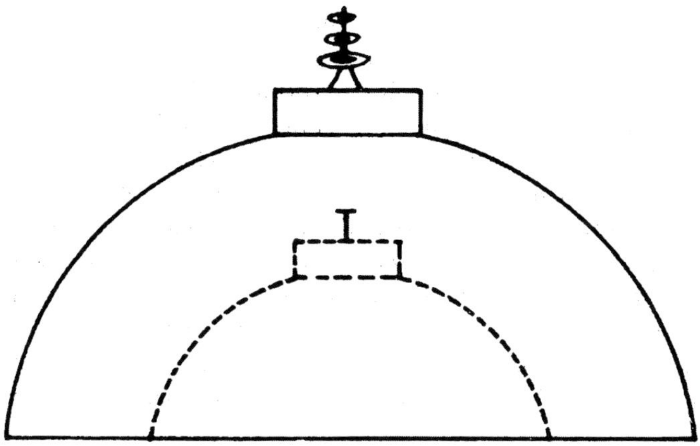

A Conjectural L.S. of the Sanchi Tope

in between.

The great stupa at Sanchi (India) is a classical example of the first type. (Fig. *76*)

The Nakorn Pathon shrine in southern Thailand provides an excellent example of a stupa encased with an empty space in between. (Fig. *117*). The inner stupa which in its initial state is said to be quite ancient, is visible through a peep hole in the encasement. Moreover, its replica is located to the south of the encased monument (Fig. *118*). As regards the multiple encasements, perhaps the *Rhwedagurṁ cetī* (Fig. *75*) of Rangoon provides about the best example. This huge and magnificent shrine, which now represents the final phase of architectural evolution in the *cetī* structure in Burma was originally of modest dimensions. According to U Aung Than:

> Up to the 14th century, little was known of the pagoda. In 1372, Binnya U, king of Hanthawaddy (Pegu) visited Dagon (Rangoon) in state and repaired the pagoda. Successive kings in Burma, Mon and Burmese, repaired or re-gilt it till the Shwedagon reached its present size... It was in the time of Shin Shinsawbu (A.D. 1455-62) that it first assumed something of its present shape and appearance... She gilded the pagoda from top to bottom with gold leaves equal to her weight. Her brother ... Binnyagyan had raised the Pagoda to a height of 302 feet ... Sinbyushin, king of Ava, raised the Pagoda to its present height in 1774 and made a new Hti ... for it, gilding it with his own weight in gold costing Rs. 94, 000... King Mindon (also made a new Hti

The story of the *Rhwedagum̐* constitutes a fascinating episode in the evolution of the *cetī* architecture in Burma. It is bound to reveal layers after layers of encasement, each layer different from the other till is reached the original *cetī*, which must have been of the type of a mound. As a matter of fact, the entire evolution of the *cetī* architecture can be envisaged through a conjectural longitudinal section of this pagoda as illustrated below:

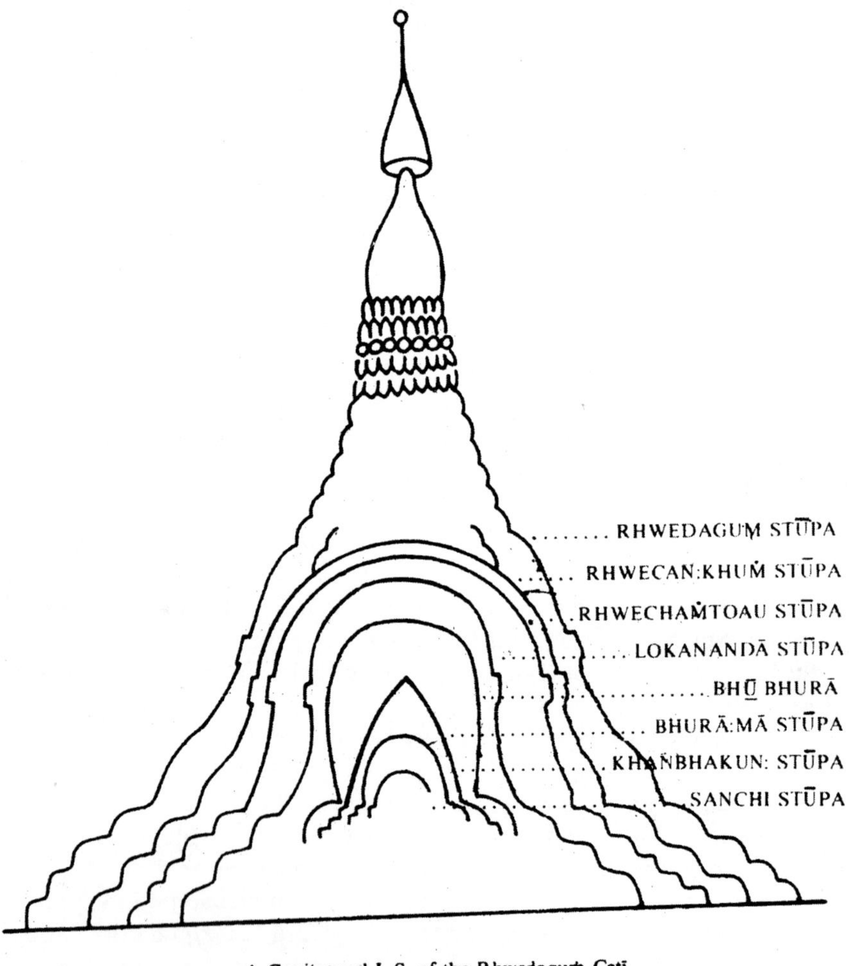

A Conjectural L.S. of the Rhwedagum̐ Cetī

Aung Than: *Shwedagon*, (Rangoon, Hanthawaddy Press, 2nd Edn. 1957), 21-2.

The architectural character of the encasement of a *cetī* is such that is not marked by a uniform process. It may be:

1. Structurally alike to the original *cetī* within, for example the Sanchi stupa in India (Fig. *76*), or
2. architecturally quite unlike the *cetī* enclosed, for example the *cetī* at Nakorn Pathom (Figs. *117* & *118*) and some *cetīs* at Pagan (Figs. *72* & *73*).

Very little or no information is available with regard to the original structures and their encasements, as met with in the case of certain pagodas on the soil of earlier Pagan (Figs. *68, 70, 71, 72* & *73*) and *Mhoaujā* (Fig. *69*). Neither their original names are known nor the names of the architects or donors nor the dates of construction of the encased structures and the encasements. Of course, the testimony of the witnesses is out of question, the structures being centuries old, with several generations of residents having passed out of existence. To come to a correct conclusion, one cannot merely depend on hearsay stories or certain data objectively in view. Regretfully enough, no inscriptions have yet been found.

On the basis of the observed facts, could, of course, be built certain theories, which, however, because of their speculative nature, would be able to offer a clear historical picture only on the availability of solid facts of inscriptional nature in the future. Whether such facts would be available or not is problematical. However, we will do well to remain optimistic and hopeful, at least so far as some of the structures are concerned. Inscriptions are the sheet-anchor of factual history: in the absence of this mainstay, the conclusions will but be provisional: this, because of the difficulties involved in the correct dating of the early structures and the later encasements, modifications or distortions.

Certainly, a wealth of material is made available, because of the painstaking researches of a long line of distinguished archaeologists, and also of eminent scholars such as G.H. Luce and Dr Than Tun. This has revealed certain vital aspects of the ancient architecture of the *cetīs* in Burma and the evolution these underwent in their structural pattern. However, many puzzles yet await research of the scientific type. In solving these puzzles in relation to the encased pagodas, the historians will have either to look for the relevant inscriptions or in the alternative, for certain materials which could be assessed with definite or near definite certainty with respect to their chronological coefficient. Of course, if the inscriptions and the materials be both available, the conclusions will be helped to be strengthened in their results, howsoever provisional for the time being.

Without emphasizing further on the need of factual research on the subject of encased pagodas, the fact, of course, needs be accepted as undeniable that the encased pagodas existed before the encasement they underwent. The question, arises as to what occasioned the need for the encasement. A solid pagoda, as is well known, in most cases has a *Dhātu-gabbha* or a reliquary or a casket with sacred relics or holy materials, the only exception to this being when a *cetī* is raised to commemorate a memorable event of religious import. Being a very precious reliquary of spiritual import, its security needs vigilant and continued attention. It was to achieve this objective to a fool-proof degree that the solid pagodas which were the repositories of the sacred relics began to be encased with massive structures. While at times the encasement was out of materials similar to the ones used in the earlier monument, at other times the encasement was out of materials stronger and more lasting than the original ones, as in the case of the great Tope at Sanchi (Fig. *76*), which got encased with stone over the original brick-built structure of half the final size. To concretize the security further, some solid pagodas got a multiplicity of encasements, as in the case of the *Rhwedaguṁ* at Rangoon. (Fig. *75*). The legendary account of the construction of the *Rhwedaguṁ cetī* has it that a vault was dug on the hill where eight hairs of the living Buddha were to be enshrined.

> (On this vault) a golden stone slab was placed... and on it was erected a golden pagoda enclosed within sliver, tin, copper, lead, marble and iron brick pagodas up to a height of 44 cubits (66 feet).[5]

A custom as this of enclosing the reliquary with layers after layers of different materials to ensure the security of the precious relics within, more or less continued through centuries. This practice, in fact assumed the status of an authoritative custom, so much so that it had to be more or less followed as a matter of established rule. And, an interesting phenomenon is that this established usage far from remaining confined to the solid pagodas or *cetīs*, extended even to the hollow pagodas. This is very well evidenced by an inscription dated A.D. 1228 (The *Maṅ:nansū Inscription*)[6] at Pagan

Translated into English, by Dr. Than Tun; it is as follows:

> We constructed a hollow-pagoda. When enshrining (that) hollow-pagoda, (we) encased the relics of the Holy Body in a sandalwood casket and put it within a crystal casket, (then) a red sandalwood casket, a gold (casket), a silver (casket), a gilt and jewelled (casket), an invory (casket), a red copper (casket) and (lastly) within a stone (miniature) pagoda.[7]

The above quotation is an important contribution to the understanding

5. Aung Than: *Shwedagon*, 21.
6. *Man:nansu Inscription*, A.D. 1228, Pl. 73, Line 8-10.

of the classical way the elements in the sacred reliquary were safeguarded. It amply testifies to the thoughtfulness exercised and planned care undertaken to ensure the security of the reliquary to the best extent possible.

A distinction needs however, be made between the intrinsic encasement mentioned above, more or less commonly practised for obvious reasons, and the extrinsic massive encasements under discussion, as seen in some of the *cetīs* in earlier Pagan (Figs. *68, 70, 71, 72* & *73*), and in *Mhoaujā* (Fig. *69*).

Besides the reasons already enumerated, another reason for such encasements could be to safeguard the architectural integrity of the original structure, which having developed cracks or some other damage such as crumblings in parts through faults in the original design or the devastations wrought by wind and weather or the destructive hands of man, needed attention. In this way, not only adequate repairs were effected, but also the repetition of the breakdown was greatly obviated. That the encased *cetī* was duly repaired before being encased is evidenced by the statement of some reputed and experienced archaeologists in Burma. That perhaps is the reason that we find the so far investigated encased *cetī* to be in a condition refreshingly complete in almost all their details.

And, yet another reason, in some cases for the encasement has been the piety of the devotees, who in the faithful observance of the religious principles, considered it highly meritorious to encase the pagoda. This, in due course, took the shape of encasing not with brick and mortar or stone or marble, but with gold leaves. No wonder, the *Rhwedagurṅ* at Rangoon, the most ancient and yet the most evolved and up to date solid shrine in Burma, has tons of gold-leaf stuck on to its surface by devotees ranging between kings and commoners of all walks of life.

There have been discovered some structures with beautiful stupas within. One such *cetī* was found at *Mhoaujā* in 1927-8 (Fig. *69*), three at *Sīripaccayā* near Pagan in 1930-1 (Figs. *70, 71* & *72*), and one at *Mrań:kapā* in 1905-6 (Fig. *73*).[8] With the exception of the encasement at *Mrań:kapā* and another at *Sīripaccayā* (Figs. *73* & *72*), which give a fairly good idea of the completed external structure, all the other three encasements were in a ruined state (Figs. *69, 70,* & *71*). However, all the five encasements were massive. While the design of the encasements at *Mhoaujā* is beyond recovery, (Fig. *69*), the encasements of the two *cetīs* at *Sīripaccayā* (Figs. *70,* & *71*), could well be imagined to be near about the magnification of the original structure: there is evidence of high

7. Than Tun: *History of Buddhism*, 131.
8. Fig. 18 representing a circular pagoda In ruins also gives the hint of having been encased.

foundation in both cases and of the bell-shaped top in one case (Fig. *71*), as evidenced by a residual section intact. Both of the encased *cetīs* are found complete in all their sections, one of them (Fig. *70*) even having a throne-shaped base with panels for Jātaka plaques. Such a throne-shaped base is also evidenced in the *cetī* at *Mhoaujā* (Fig. *69*). The bell is well formed in both cases and the mouldings of the spires are found executed with perfect dexterity, ending in finials without umbrella—an architectural feature marking the finality of the *cetī* architecture during the Pagan Period. The crowning with the umbrella and other adornments at the top, as seen in the *Rhwedagum̊* at Rangoon, are features peculiar to the post Pegan Period. These features came to Pagan to adorn its pagodas after its fall. Otherwise, the final architectural style at Pagan was with a rounded finial (Figs. *51, 52, 53* & *54*). In these four pagodas, fortunately enough, the restoration is in accord with the original style.

When the architectural character of the encasement of a *cetī* is in accord with the structure within, the situation is quite understandable in the light of the observations made earlier. The encased *cetīs* at *Sīripaccayā* (Figs. *70* & *71*) and that at *Mrañ:kapā* (Fig. *68*) come under this category. As regards the *Mrañ:kapā cetī*, though the upper part of it is missing, it is unmistakably on a high platform and its contour could be conjectured to be that of early bell-shape. Also, when the encasement is a definite departure in design and dimensions from the *cetī* encased, but of a character marked by further evolutionary progress in the architectural field, the situation can even then be well accepted as an older *cetī* being encased by a comparatively better evolved structure, with a view to save it not only from the state of disrepair but also to give to it a touch of modernity. However, the situation gets into a confounded state when the encased *cetī* is discovered to be of a design bespeaking of a fully developed evolutionary touch in contrast to the comparatively crude encasement without.

On studying the two pagodas with more or less very well defined encasements (Figs. *72* & *73*), we come face to face with a serious architectural challenge. While the encased one in one case (Fig. *72*) shows only its top and the other (Fig. *73*) is more or less in view, both give the idea of being fully evolved structures, so far as the Pagan Period is concerned. However, the encasements, though massive, are architecturally contrary to the *cetīs* encased. While in one case (Fig. *73*), the foundation and terraces, though high and broadbased, are in an utterly ruined state, in the other case (Fig. *72*) the foundation is peculiarly laid, it tapering down centripetally. This reminds us of a somewhat similar structure of a solid brick-work temple at Bhitargaon in Cawnpore district in North India (Fig. *135*). According to Cunningham, it could be of the 4th or 5th century A.D.[9] Besides the tapering inwards at the base in the case of the Pagan *cetī* (Fig. *72*), the terraces rise in a way as if the construction was not meant for circumambulation. And, the most peculiar thing is that the encasing pagoda at the top in one case (Fig. *72*) gives the impression of being more or less after the *Nakywainātoṅ* model (Fig. *28*), though unlike the latter, perched very high, and the encasing *cetī* in the other case (Fig. *73*) seems to be more or less an architectural imitation of the *Lokanandā* (Fig. *21*).

In the light of the above factual observations, the question arises as to why the fully evolved *cetīs* suffered encasements of the type which could architecturally, from the evolutionary point of view, be characterized as retrograde. While an encasement of a progressive nature is easily understandable a retrograde step in the field of encasement needs a satisfactory explanation. Of course, it would be simply silly to accept that models depicting forms after the *Bhū Bhurā:*, the *Lokanandā* or the *Ṅakywainātoṅ cetīs* (Figs. *17, 21* & *28*) were improvements upon the final stage in *cetī* architecture reached during the Pagan Period. However, the fact remains, as testified to by these two *cetīs* that some of the final models in quite a fine form were encased with structures of primitive type. This reminds us of a phenomenon well known in the sphere of biological evolution, going by the name of atavism, which sets into action a tendency for the recurrence of an ancestral type or of such a trait, after the lapse of some generations. Could it be that the people began to look back with adoration on their cultural heritage of the past and as such designed encasements of certain *cetīs* to get enthused on the objective realization of such an aspiration? It might be that such encasements were effected under the patronage of people who were inspired by their past history.

As to when the encasement of decently executed lovely *cetīs* took place, it is not difficult to arrive at a probable conclusion. In view of the fact that all the encased *cetīs* found in Pagan and Prome zones were of the later Pagan Period type, the hypothesis is obvious that these got encased at or soon after the fall of the Pagan Dynasty. Could it be that the invasion of the Mongols initiated a move to save some *cetīs* by hurried encasements of any sort? A theory as this gains support from the fact that certain large Buddha images of solid gold in some places, particularly in Thailand, were in dangerous times of war and devastation, encased with thick plaster and thus successfully saved from the greedy eyes of the looters and the destructive hands of the invaders. Or, could it be that the donor (i.e., paya-daga or paya-dagama) of the *cetī*, after constructing the original shrine, in due course snowballed into affluence, which gave him

9. Ḥasan, Yakub: *Temples, Churches & Mosques*, (Madras, G.A. Natesan & Co., 1926), 59.

or her a sense of indebtedness, to discharge which the encasement was effected out of the surplus wealth available? Or, if not the original donor, others, impelled by a sense of piety, might have brought about the encasement out of the surplus funds with them as is usually the case with most of the encasements, as exemplified by the history of the *Rhwedagum̀ cetī.*

The solid pagodas being the repositories of sacred and also precious elements, their preservation becomes a matter of religious merit. Moreover, these *cetīs* besides being architectural monuments, they merit to be kept safe from dilapidation in order to be maintained as pieces symbolic of the national culture. It is to meet these ends that shrines of particular historical value are occasionally submitted to the act of restoration through requisite repairs, which makes them retain, so far as possible, their original design in most cases. However, exception to this are witnessed when persons out of misplaced enthusiasm for repairs bring harm to the structure. Also, harm may occur through treasure hunters and curio-collectors. To obviate such unfortunate events, the authorities in Burma, through the Cultural Ministry, have been looking after certain structures of historical and cultural value on the soil of Pagan as also in other places in the country: this, in spite of the meaningless current superstition that there was no merit in repairing old shrines, a superstition which possibly took birth after the fall of Pagan. Besides the safety of the enshrined elements ensured through layer after layer of different materials over the reliquary, and the timely attention paid to the *cetī* through repairs, which keep up the architectural integrity of the shrine, the security is further ensured through the process of encasement of the *cetī*. Such an encasement is met with in some *cetīs* on the soil of Pagan. The encasement is architecturally either similar to the one encased or otherwise: also, while mostly the encasement fits tightly over the encased structure, in some instances it is with a space between the two. The encased *cetīs* at Pagan, in the absence of any inscriptional or other positive data, present certain problems connected with their encasements. It might be that these encasements if not conducted earlier to save the structure from ruin, or to enlarge it as an act of merit, were executed in the wake of the Mongol invasion to safeguard these *cetīs* against pillage, as was done to ensure the security of some gold images through a cover of plaster in Thailand in times of war.

CHAPTER V

A Comparative Look at Neighbouring Countries

Part I
India and Ceylon

The period covered by the Pagan Dynasty, starting with *Aniruddha* (A.D. 1044) and ending with *Tarukpliy* in A.D. 1287, is a period of vital importance, among other things, for the history of pagoda architecture in Burma. While qualitatively, the solid pagodas, presently the theme of our study, passed through evolutionary phases which gave a distinctive Burmese character to the *cetī* architecture, quantitatively the area covered by the ancient city of Pagan can well be regarded as unique the world over for the number of religious shrines per square mile on its bosom. The materials available at Pagan though grand and richly magnificent even in their present ruined state, evidence inspiration from earlier structures in the country, particularly at *Śrī Kṣetra*, which in turn in its building activity was markedly influenced by architectural developments in India, the birthplace of Buddhist architecture in history.

It was from India that the art of architecture, as applied to Buddhist shrines and other religious edifices, spread out to other countries with the spread of Buddhism over there. However, notwithstanding the fact that though the basic principles of the monumental mound or a *thūpa* i.e., stupa, which forms the central structure of a *cetī* or solid pagoda, were accepted by the new converts for the construction of shrines in their lands, the shape these edifices took in form, design, mouldings, decorations and adjuncts more or less varied from country to country. These were expressive of the inner feelings of the persons concerned, feelings bearing the impress of their native culture and traditional sense of beauty and harmony. It was this that made Pagan the paradise of the Burmese art: also, it was this that made the Burmese pagoda a distinctive piece of art when compared with the Buddhist shrines in the neighbouring countries, including India, wherefrom the initial stimulus came to raise such shrines.

It will be of interest to cast our gaze back to the period 11th-13th centuries, and look at the contemporary developments in the field of religious architecture as applied to the temples, mostly in countries neighbouring Burma, such as India, Ceylon, Thailand, Cambodia and Indonesia, also those in the Himalayan and trans-Himalayan regions. This covers quite a vast field, for, each country contributed in its own way and thus enriched the religious architecture markedly. The complex background—cultural, economic, social, political and religious—of this development is a subject in itself for a number of theses. Suffice it to here sketch the fundamental issues relating to our subject.

With the advent of Asoka, Buddhist architecture took a definite course in India, with the stupa as the centre of worship. The stupa at Sanchi, originally built by Asoka in 250 B.C. and enlarged a century later, is a sterling example of the stupa architecture of the time (Fig. *76*). Its Northern Gateway (Fig. *78*) ascribed to first century B.C. is a distinctive contribution to the Buddhist art. Though the Sanchi Tope represents the earliest phase of solid *cetīs* in the history of the Buddhist art, notwithstanding the evolutionary growth in the *cetī* architecture in later ages, the surprising thing is that its design did not lose fascination with the people. For, as late as A.D. 1648, i.e., some nineteen centuries after the Sanchi Tope was raised in India, King Thalun of Burma constructed a massive stupa by the name of *Koṅ:mhutoau* (Fig. *7*) at Sagaing in Upper Burma, after the model of the *Mahācetī* at Anuradhapura (Ceylon), which architecturally was but a reproduction of the design of the Sanchi Tope in India (Fig. *76*). Also, mention may be made that Asoka, besides the Sanchi Tope and numerous other Buddhist monuments in India, built "the original *Mahā Bodhi* Temple"[1] at Bodhgaya (India). The present structure (Fig. *81*), however, is a later construction, for, the Temple in between suffered repeatedly from decay and destruction, needing periodic attention. In this connection it is worthy of note that in the 11th century *Thiluiṅ Maṅ* of Pagan (Burma) conducted extensive repairs to this historic Temple. A little over 125 miles from Bodhgaya is Sarnath, where the Buddha delivered His first Sermon. This town has an interesting massive stupa, the Dhamek Stupa (Fig. *84*), which is said to be at the site "where Lord Buddha prophesied the coming of the future Buddha Maitriya."[2] Mention may also be made here of two Buddhist temples of peculiar architectural style in Northern India. One is the two storeyed brick-built temple, dated 4th. century A.D., at Bhitargaon (Fig. *135*) in Cawnpore district, with a peculiar

1. Cunningham, A. : *Mahābodhi*, (Varanasi , Indological Book House, 1892), 77.
2. Valisinha, Devapriya: *Buddhist Shrines in India* (Colombo, The Maha Bodhi Society of Ceylon, 1948), 70.

shape somewhat simulating the encasement of a Pagan *cetī* (Fig. *72*). Another is an ancient shrine at Nalanda (Fig. *136*), which multi-storeyed rises tower-like, with the Buddha images installed in the niches all around. Some structure as this was in all probability the prototype of multi-storeyed and other tall structures for the Buddha images in Thailand [Figs. *114, 119, 120-(1)* & *(6)*]. Also, it might have given to the Chinese pilgrims the idea of using their towers as image-houses (Figs. *102* & *103*).

Besides the stupa in the open, another development between 2nd century B.C. and 2nd century A.D., was that of stupa established in caves hewn out of the living rocks. A representative example of these in the Western Ghats is in the group of stupas around Nasik, the stupa at Karle (Fig. *79*) being an excellent member of these. In the meantime, in the early centuries of the Christian era, there were interesting developmets in the North-West, where the Gandhara art had taken birth. Of this, regrettably enough, the famous majestic Tower of Kanishka at Peshawar is utterly lost. However, there are still in existence remains of over fifteen topes which give an excellent account of themselves. Of these, the Manikyala Tope—1st. century A.D. and the model of a *cetī* found in a tope at Manikyala—beginning of the Christian Era (Fig. *85*) are excellent examples of the structural development of the period in the field of Buddhist architecture. The Gupta Period (A.D. 350-650) that followed, imparted a new orientation to the situation. The Gupta Art, apart from exercising fascination over the native mind, provided models for countries abroad.

> The sculptures of the Malay Peninsula, Sumatra, Java, Annam, Cambodia and even Celebes bear the indelible stamp of Gupta art.[3]

While these developments were in progress in the North, Southern India went on independently evolving the temple architecture along lines distinctive. From 200 B.C. to 4th century A.D., Buddhist fanes rose in profusion in the Lower Valley of the Krishna river, at Amaravati (Fig. *80*) and Nagarjunakonda. In later periods, there arose Chalukyan temples (A.D. 450-750) mostly devoted to Hinduism. However, there also arose Pallava Buddhist shrines, mostly around Conjeeveram (A.D. 600-900). Of course, the Pallavas too, not unlike the Guptas, had their share in spreading Indian architecture abroad.

> The characteristic Pallava or Dravidian type of Sikhara is met with in the temples of Java, Cambodia and Annam. But there are important differences between them and the South Indian temples. The Pillars which form such an important adjunct to the

3. Majumdar et. al: *History*, 238.

latter are altogether absent in the former.[4]

The Hindu temple architecture in the South, however, reached its culmination under the Cholas (A.D. 900-1150) who supplanted the Pallavas. The best example of this new development is provided by the Brihadesvara Śiva Temple at Tanjore (Fig. *87*). Its great Sikhara of fourteen storeys rising to a height of 190' is crowned with a massive stone dome. Besides, a new development in the Chola art was the addition of a huge gateway, called Gopuram, to the enclosure of the temple. The Suchendram Temple at Travancore (South India) provides a good example of such a gateway (Fig. *88*). It may also be observed that the Hoysalas or the later Chalukyas who ruled over the Mysore plateau in the 11th to 13th centuries A.D., contemporaneous with the Pagan Period, evolved a new style of architecture, wherein the temples assumed polygonal or star-shaped forms (Fig. *90*). Moreover, the Sikhara in these is pyramidal but low. The Cholas were succeeded by the Pandyas. They were, however, not important from our point of view, their's being not a notable building dynasty. In power from the 12th to the 14th centuries, they gave way to the Vijayanager Dynasty which lasted till 1565.

In the meantime, there were new developments in the North under *Indo-Aryan* architecture, covering the period. A.D. 800 to 1250. Noteworthy examples of these are witnessed scattered all over Northern India. In the east, in Orissa, there were the temples such as the Jagannath at Puri (which originally is said to have been a Buddhist shrine), the Surya Temple of A.D. 1250 at Konarak, the Raja-Rani Temple at Bhubaneswar—c. A.D. 1000, and the Lingaraja Temple, also at Bhubaneswar—c. A.D. 1000. In Central India, near Jhansi there is the Khajuraho group of thirty Hindu temples (A.D. 950-1050), which are richly decorated with sculpture. The largest of the entire group is the Śiva Temple of Kandariya Mahadeo—c. A.D. 1000. Besides, there were other noteworthy temples in Rajputana, the one at Osia in Marwar, c. 10th century, (Fig. *89*) being a good example of these. Its Sikhara is architecturally somewhat similar to the ones crowning the hollow temples in Pagan. Further West, Gujarat too had magnificent Hindu temples, the Surya Temple there at Modhera dated A.D. 1026-7, being

> still a monument of incomparable beauty...
> (with) an atmosphere of spiritual grace.[5]

Of the Northern or Indo-Aryan type of temples, two more merit special mention. They are the Gondeswara Temple at Sinner in Nasik district of 12th century A.D., and the grand, magnificently decorated larger Sas Bahu Temple of the 11th century A.D. (Fig. *91*).

4. Majumdar et. al: *History*, 249.
5. Brown: *Architecture*, 146-7.

The Indian temple architecture, broadly speaking, is distinguishable into two styles, the Indo-Aryan—Northern and the Dravidian—Southern. The difference lies mainly in the shape of their Sikharas.

> The Northern Indian Sikhara has the appearance of a solid mass of curvilinear tower, bulging in the middle and ending in almost a point (Fig. *86*). The South-Indian sikhara... looks like a pyramid made up of successive storeys each smaller than and receding a little from the one beneath it (Fig. *87*).[6]

Moreover, while in the South Indian temples pillars play an important part, they are absent in the North Indian structures. Leaving the pillars apart, the Sikhara architecture calls for a comment here. For, this new development in India found its way into Pagan, where the hollow temples, viz., the *Thīlui Maṅlui,* the *Ananda,* the *Kanto, pallaṅ,* the *Sabaññu,* the *Rhwekūkrī*: and the *Bhurā:sum:chū* Temples at Pagan (Figs. *57, 15, 32, 56, 60* & *65*), came to be adorned with sikharas, but in their own distinctive Burmese way. Even the *Ānanda* Temple, which is said to have been built in imitation of the cave-temple of Ananta in the Udayagiri hills of Orissa, might not be with a slavish imitation of the sikhara there. For, as suggested by Serge S.Ozhegov, the sikharas at Pagan are not to be considered as mere imitation of the Indian architecture. Pointing out the difference, he observes:

> The Indian Sikhara is an independent architectural-sculptural form, standing on the ground or on low pedestal,... while the Pagan Sikhara is the top element of a big building: it is not the basic part but only one of the elements of the whole composition.[7]

Of course, taking Sikhara in itself, there are noticeable similarities, the Sikhara of the Kangra Temple—c. A.D. 1200 (Fig. *86*), being found structurally nearer to those of the Pagan temples than other Sikharas in Northern India.

From the observations made above, it is obvious that the religious architecture passed through diverse phases in different parts of India. Though originally initiated under Buddhist auspices, the architecture did not fail to come under Hindu influences with the latter's return to power. Another feature that cannot pass unnoticed is that while Burma under the Pagan Dynasty (A D. 1044-1287) was hectically busy in the raising of the Buddhist shrines, India was not able to keep up such an enthusiasm exclusively in favour of Buddhism at the time. This for twofold reason. Firstly, Buddhism in India after a prolonged encounter with Brahminism for centuries and cloistered but luxurious retreat had lost its original

6. Majumdar, et. al.: *History*, 244.
7. Ozhegov, Serge S.: "Originality of Burmese Architecture," F, II, ix, Dec. 7, 1963, 19.

vigor, which made it hard for it to argue back with the neo-Hindu intellectual giants. Secondly, with the Muslim invasion in the early 11th century A.D. and the occupation of the land in the 13th century A.D., most of the Buddhist instiutions got razed to the ground.

> (Pathetically enough), the monastery of Bihar, in the Patna district, was sacked and its monks slaughtered by the invaders under the mistake that they were soldiers.[8]

Hinduism too suffered no less in the North through the Muslim conquerors.

> From inscriptional evidence it is known that twenty-six temples were dismantled to provide materials for the Delhi mosque (which had 240 pillars and the)... Ajmir mosque...(which had) 235 pillars.[9]

While pillage and destruction as the above despoiled the treasures of art in the north and put the hands of time back with respect to the Buddhist and Hindu architecture for a considerable time, the building activity south of the Vindhya range continued more or less unhindered for some time. It was mostly from there and also to an extent from the easternmost section of India under the Palas, that influences in the field of art and architecture continued to flow to lands beyond the Indian borders.

While India mostly ceased to be the source of new ideological and artistic inspiration to foreign lands after the 12th century, the religious thought and artistic skill already gone abroad continued to grow there, under native patronage, taking nationalized forms. The architectural glory of the Pagan Period in Burma amply testifies to this fact. Also, Ceylon, being so near to India, had imbibed much and quite early from her in the sphere of architecture.

The early Buddhist architecture in Ceylon bears a great resemblance to the contemporary Indian structures.

> The oldest Buddhist edifice found in Ceylon is the *stūpa* (Pali: *thūpa*, Sinhalese:*dāgaba*)... The oldest dagaba...is the Thūparama dagaba in Anuradhapura built by king Devanampiyatissa (250-210 B.C.), the first Buddhist king (in Ceylon).[10]

The dagabas of Ceylon bear diverse forms, namely bell-shaped, pot-shaped, bubble-shaped, and paddy-heap-shaped, among others. (Fig. *92*).

> (The dagaba), ordinarily semi-globular in form,... stands on a range of concentric circular platforms almost invariably three in number, the whole based on a square terrace approached by a

8. Sarkar, J.: *India Through the Ages*, (Calcutta, 1950), 388.
9. Brown: *Architecture*, 139.
10. Godakumbura, C.E.: *Sinhalese Architecture*, (Colombo, Department of Cultural Affairs, 1963), 4. Hereafter this work will be referred to as Godakumbura: *Architecture*.

> flight of steps in the middle of each side. Over the summit of the dome arose the finial consisting of a box-like member in which valuable offerings were placed, previous to the *chattravali* or conventional parasol being erected, as a spire, crowning the whole.[11]

In view of the Pagan Period being the object of our study, we will do well to understand the contemporary developments in pagoda architecture in Ceylon by a look at Polonnaruwa, which was the capital after Anuradhapura, from the 8th to the 13th centuries A.D.

> Polonnaruwa...in the twelfth century became not only a city of marked architectural grandeur, but it was significant of a movement of great importance in the history of the building art in Ceylon.[12]

The Kirivehara (Fig. *93*) built by king Parakramabahu (A.D. 1153-86), and the Rankotvehara built by the next king Nissankamalla (A.D. 1187-96) were massive structures. Also, Wata Dage (Fig. *95*) built by Parakrama the Great, is an architectural structure of a notably graceful kind. According to Fergusson,

> (this) circular building, which, so far as is at present known, is all but unique.[13]

There were other dagabas too belonging to the period, the highest being the Yudaganava dagaba in the *south* 180 feet in height. An interesting feature is that walls of the relic-chambers in some dagabas were found with paintings depicting incidents from the life of the Buddha. The Mahiyangana dagaba of about the 12th century had these. However, after the 12th century, no large dome-shaped dagabas were built. Their dimensions gradually decreased and "the bell-shaped dagabas became the most popular."[14]

A distinct contribution, however, which Ceylon made to the Buddhist architecture was what came to be known as Asanaghara or buildings housing the replica of the Bodhi throne of the Buddha. There were also image-houses of bricks: the one of many such built by Parakramabahu in the 12th century is at Polonnaruwa, named Thuparama. Also, built in his reign at the place was Lankatilaka or Jetawanarama, the largest and loftiest brick image-house (Fig. *96*). This temple is a typical example of having colossal figures of the Buddha,

> constructed entirely of brick covered with stucco, even the statue of the Buddha which is nearly sixty feet high in the interior being

11. Brown: *Architecture*, 202.
12. Brown: *Architecture*, 207.
13. Fergusson: *History*, 247.
14. Godakumbura: *Architecture*, 6.

> built up by the same process.[15]

Also, in the same zone are met with two-floor image-houses, the upper storey being for the Tooth. One of such is Atadage built by Vijayabahu I (A.D. 1056-1111) and the other is the Hatadage built by Nissankamalla (A.D. 1187-96). Moreover, there still exists the ancient temple of the Tooth at Dambadeniya, built by king Parakramabahu II (A.D. 1236-70), now used as image house.

Of course, Buddhism in Ceylon suffered much at the hands of the ruthless invaders. These were the Cholas from South India. They in the 11th century imposed on the people Hindu ideas and architecture. However, Ceylon outlived these ravages, after Vijayabahu restored Singhalese sovereignty.

Another noteworthy feature in the Singhalese Buddhist architecture is that the two-storeyed temple led to the evolution of a shrine on pillars in the later centuries (Fig. *94*). These pillars, whether of stone or wood, had at times exquisite carvings. The ascent to the building was through flight of steps flanked by well-designed balustrades, the first step being reached by a slab of 'moon-stone' in half-moon form, well patterned and carved (Fig. *97*). Mention needs be made that in Burmese architecture, only a specimen bearing the semblance of a 'Moon-Stone' has been dicovered at the ancient site of *Bissaṇui*: Also, some monasteries in Burma are found to have a modified form of it. (See illustration No. 97 Part II)

There is another feature of note in the Singhalese Buddhist architecture. That is that while the bell-shaped stupa finally attained favour with the people as in Burma, its adornments and beautifying mouldings were mostly left out, unlike in Burma.

> (For unlike the Pagan *cetīs* or) the Indian stupas, as for instance Amaravati or Sanchi, the Sinhalese dagabas were not highly decorated works of architecture.[16]

Unlike at Pagan, where we come across no solid remains of impressive 'Sabbath Halls' or *uposathāgāra*, these are met with in Ceylon, the remains of such a structure near the Mahavihara at Anuradhapura being a good example: hailed as Lovamahapaya or the Brazen Palace and built by king Dutugemunu, it was finally renovated by king Parakramabahu of Polonnaruwa.

> The edifice is described in the chronicles as being originally built of nine storeys with hundred chambers in each storey. The architectural embellishments of the building were of the costliest character and its wooden roof was covered with gilt copper-tiles.[17]

15. Brown: *Architecture*, 207.
16. Brown: *Architecture*, 203.
17. Godakumbura: *Architecture*, 20-1.

Even there are, unlike at Pagan, examples of the royal palaces, council chambers and audience halls, in Ceylon of the 12th century. This might be because these structures were partly of 'indestructible granite which, although damaged, still remains in situ."[18] There were also baths built of stone, the remains of which give an eloquent account of the sanitary sense possessed by the people, who were skilled not only in the construction of huge artificial lakes but also in the effective system of drainage.

Peculiarly enough, Polonnaruwa and Pagan provide an interesting but tragic historical parallel. While Pagan was invaded by the Mongols,

> Polonnaruwa was abandoned at the close of the thirteenth century, and the arts consequently suffered a considerable interval of decline, only to be revived when Kandy became the seat of the Sinhalese monarchy from 1592 to 1815.[19]

In Burma too, there was a considerable, though not absolute, set-back in the building and other arts, after the fall of the Pagan Dynasty till the rise of the *Kun:bhoṅ* Dynasty in A.D. 1752 under *Aloṅmaṅ:tarā:*. He once more succeeded in bringing entire Burma under one rule. The city of Mandalay, the last capital under the Dynasty, in a little over a quarter century (A.D. 1857-85) of its royal existence, got adorned with magnificent structures of artistic glory and architectural splendour, some of which still exist and the description of many is available in a number of publications.[20],[21],[22] & [23]. However, the historical parallel between Ceylon and Burma found its culmination in the tragic fact that while Kandy, the last seat of the Singhalese monarchy fell in 1815, Mandalay, the last seat of the Burmese monarchy fell in 1885, and both to the British, whose rule ended almost near about the same time in 1948 with the regaining of independence by both the countries after the World War II.

Part II
Contemporary Developments in the Himalayan and the Trans-Himalayan regions

With the Pagan Period in Burma as the object of our study, it has been quite instructive to note the contemporary developments in shrine architecture between 11th to 13th centuries in India and Ceylon. These are the two countries where not unlike Burma solid pagodas more or less continued to appeal to the religious sense of the people throughout the

18. Brown: *Architecture*, 201.
19. Brown: *Architecture*, 208.
20. Than Tun: " History of Mandalay," *AM*, I,1968-9, 200-1.
21. Duroiselle, C.: *Guide to the Mandalay Palace*, (Calcutta, Government of India, Central Publication Branch, 1931).
22. *Mandalay Palace*: (Directorate of Archaeological Survey, Ministry of Union Culture, 1963)
23. *Mandalay and Environs*, (Ministry of Union Culture, Government of the Union of Burma).

ages. On looking around in the 11th to 13th centuries, we find the Buddhist fanes scattered all over the place near and around Burma. Not only in the Himalayan states, but also in China, Korea and Japan the developments were significant. Moreover, the Sino-Burmese block of land, now divided into Thailand, Cambodia, Laos and Vietnam presents magnificent specimens of religious architecture. Besides, the countless islands in the Pacific and even beyond merit a look around.

It is certain that Buddhism reached Central Asia and China quite early, the first monastery in Khotan in Sinkiang having been built in 211 B.C.

> The tradition further claims that an Indian dynasty ruled Khotan for 56 generations during which Buddhism continued to be the dominant religion of the state.[24]

The Chinese annals of the 3rd century A.D. are eloquent of nearly a thousand stupas and temples in the Kucha area of Sinkiang. The Chinese pilgrims also testify to the flourishing state of Buddhism at Bamian (Afganistan) and in Khotan about the 7th century. For example Hiuen-Tsang (7th century A.D.) while passing through Central Asia on his way to and back from India, noted the dominance of Buddhism and Indian culture over this wide area. This is further testified by archaeological finds. However, even after the decline of the Khotan and Kucha states,

> Buddhism... (continued to be) patronized till the 11th century A.D. by the Uighur Turks who had their capital in the Turfan region (of Sinkiang).[25]

However, the conditions changed in another hundred years. The Buddhist art of Central Asia ends with the advance of Mohammedanism.

> The Uighur civilization in this region was finally overwhelmed by the Mongol invasion of Genghis Khan in the twelfth century.[26]

In contrast, that was the time when Burma was hectically busy in her enthusiasm for Buddhism and the erection of architectural monuments in its veneration.

China proper itself received Buddhism through the Sinkiang zone in the 1st century B.C. Nevertheless, Buddhism had to contend with the indigenous religion and ideas and as such faced ups and downs in its career. However, as Buddhism possessed a much profounder philosophy than Taoism and Confucianism, it soon attracted the Chinese.

There was a regular two-way traffic both by land and sea between India and China, of Indian scholars and Chinese pilgrims. Fa-hien and

24. Bapat, P.V.: *2500 Years of Buddhism*, (Delhi, Ministry of Information and Broadcasting, Reprinted 1959), 66. Hereafter this work will be referred to as Bapat: *Buddhism*.
25. Bapat: *Buddhism*, 67.
26. Rowland, Benjamin: *The Art and Architecture of India*, (England, Harmondsworth, 1954), 109. Hereafter this work will be referred to as Rowland: *Art & Architecture*.

Hiuen-Tsang among others are well known names from the Chinese side and the name of Bodhidharma is a venerated representation of the Indian scholars who visited China. While Hiuen-Tsang established a Buddhist school of thought after what he had learnt at Nalanda in India, Bodhidharma (5th century) became the founder of Ch'an School (later called Zen in Japan) in China. Several other schools of thought also came into being in China as a result of Indo-Chinese intercourse. Thus Buddhism continued to prosper in China till the 11th century A.D., the time when the Pagan Dynasty under *Aniruddha* made its start in Burma.

Surprisingly enough, while the Chinese province of Sinkiang had been rich in Buddhist architecture from early times i.e., 3rd century B.C., China proper had very little of religious architecture till later centuries, when great works of art were produced. This is well evidenced by the large color plates[27] from all over China, wherein the influence of the Gandhara school and the Gupta art is unmistakable. Even though the Temple of Heaven or the Great Dragon, the most magnificent temple in the metropolis, is said to have come into being only in the early years of the 15th century (Fig. *100*),

> substantial remains of seventh, eighth and ninth century wooden architecture in the Chinese style have been preserved in Japan.[28]

Of course, architecture had the status of a well established art in China about the time the Burmese architecture was taking its birth at Pagan. In this connection it is of interest to note that Wheeler mentions of the presentation to the throne in A.D. 1100 (Sung Dynasty 960-1279), "the first comprehensive treatise on architecture."[29] This work was printed in 1103 and again in 1145. Earlier to the 7th century too there must have been structures but mostly made of perishable materials. That the use of bricks was not unknown at the time is evidenced by the Pagoda of the Sung Yueh Temple, dated A.D. 523 (Fig. *102*), which is reputed to be the oldest brick building in China.

Most of the temples in China have a hall with diverse statues followed by a building with three images of the Buddha-triad, with another building in the rear. The latter contains a miniature dagaba, generally in marble, with relics of the Buddha enshrined in it. Of course, solid temples, except of the type of the miniature dagaba mentioned above, are not to be found as isolated pieces of Buddhist architecture, nor in forms magnificent or proportions grand anywhere in China. This is to be expected in view of the Chinese psychology, which makes them offer

---

27. The Chinese Buddhist Association: (Peking, Nationalities Publishing House, 1955).
28. Wheeler, Mortimer (Etd.): *Splendours of the East*, (London, Weidenfeld and Nicolson, 1965), 213 Hereafter this work will be referred to as Wheeler: *Splendours*.
29. Wheeler: *Splendours*, 213.

quite a reverence to their dead.

> In consequence of this, their tombs are not only objects of care, but have frequently more ornament bestowed upon them than graces the dwellings of the living.[30]

Most of these tombs are either mere conical mounds of earth with stones around the base (Fig. *99*) or dome-topped earthen mounds looking like stupas (Fig. *138*). When the rock is to be had, the tombs are cut there. Among the tombs, the tumulus type is common, one of the finest example of this being the tomb of Yunglo of the Ming Dynasty near Peking, dated A.D. 1425. Even then none of these tombs in China compare well with those found in India of the Moguls, in Samarkand and in Egypt. Obviously, the glazed dome of Tamerlane's tomb in Samarkand, the Taj Mahal at Agra and the Egyptian pyramids are highly imposing pieces of tomb architecture.

Though stupa architecture in its own right seems to have had not much of an appeal to the Chinese, tall towers hailed as pagodas, nine to thirteen storeys high, are commonly met with throughout China. Architecturally different from the Buddhist temples in other places, these so-called pagodas today are generally with the statue of the Buddha in the lower storey: above they have sometimes balconies to be used as watch towers. The one at Ningpo measures 160 feet, and another at Nankin, constructed in 1412-31, called the Porcelain Tower, is 236 feet in height (Fig. *103*). It might be mentioned here that towers were not unknown in India. A lovely example, contemporaneous with the Pagan Period, is that of the Tower of the Jainas at Chitor of the 12th century (Fig. *105*). Also, when the Pagan Empire flourished in Burma, there arose at Delhi in India the famous tower Qutb Minar in 1231-32, under the patronage of the Turkish ruler there (Fig. *104*).

These towers in China, though named pagodas, are with their origin obscure. Whatever their origin, in purpose a watch tower, an astronomical observatory, a treasury, or a minaret, these towers in some form or another, it seems, were in China from very early date, as testified to by the Sung Yueh Temple of the 6th century A.D. (Fig. *102*). It might be that these towers, initially set up for some secular purpose, began to be used as image houses after the return home of the Chinese pilgrims from India with the Buddha-images in their luggage. An ancient tower at Nalanda (India) as shown in Fig. *136*, used for the Buddha-images, might have given the idea initially of installing the images in the towers already existing in China, which in consequence began to be hailed as pagodas, a designation which continues todate. This religious use of the towers in China reminds us of the towers or minarets attached to the mosques at

---

30. Fergusson: *History II*, 465.

Samara near Baghdad, where in the 9th century, the grandson of the famous Harun-al-Rashid constructed one 160 feet high with spiral passage winding round it going up (Fig. *101*).

> (Nevertheless), there are no examples in China with external winding paths or flights of steps, these latter are usually enclosed within the brick walls.[31]

Another structure of magnificence met with in China is the gateway to a temple or a tomb. The one at a Pagoda in Peking is quite impressive (Fig. *98*). This gateway though a later development, gives a fair idea of the usual mode of constructing gateways in China. Though the Sanchi Tope in India had its own distinctive gateway as early as the 2nd century B.C. (Fig. *78*), the Chinese is a nationalized evolution of that structure. These gateways took their own forms in different lands, as Gopurams in India (Fig. *88*) and as Torii in Japan [Fig. *111 (2)*]. However, the Burmese architecture did not seem to be much interested in the elaboration of gateways.

Notwithstanding the flourishing state of Buddhism in the two great neighbouring lands, namely India and China, Tibet only broke from its isolation about the mid-seventh century, when under Sron-btsang-gampo (A.D. 629-50), Buddhism got officially introduced into the land. However, as observed by P.V. Bapat:

> Cultural contacts of Tibet with the Buddhist world surrounding her, namely, India, Khotan, Mongolia, China and Burma, must, however, have been established at least two centuries before him.[32]

However, the credit of officially ushering in Buddhism into Tibet goes to Sron-btsang-gampo, who wonderfully enough was a contemporary of Prophet Mohammad, Emperor Harsha of India and of the Chinese pilgrim Hiuen-Tsang To this may be added that it was also the time when the present era of Burma took birth in the pre-*Aniruddha* Pagan in A.D. 638. King Gampo is said to have built the Labrang monastery in the centre of Lhasa (A.D. 644). Also, his Chinese queen erected the Ramoche Temple (c.650) at Labrang to enshrine the famous sandal-wood images of Śākyamuni and Ānanda.

With all the noble efforts of King Gampo, the native animistic beliefs and superstitions stood in the way of Buddhism, which only in the 11th century may be said to have truly become the national religion of Tibet. This was through Atisa (A.D. 1038), a great scholar of Vikramasila University in India. After that Buddhism struck deep roots in Tibetan soil. The monastery at Sakya near Shigatse was founded in A.D. 1071.

31. Fergusson: *History II*, 469.
32. Bapat: *Buddhism*, 74.

The establishment is said to contain the largest single building in Tibet: It is seven storeys high, and has a spacious assembly hall.[33] The first monk-king, though yet without the title of Dalai Lama, was a Head Lama (A.D. 1235-80), whom the Chinese Emperor Kublai Khan honoured. And, the first monk-king with the title of Lama lived in A.D. 1543-88. The title of Dalai Lama combines in one person the temporal and spiritual authority. He is believed to be the living incarnation of Avalokitesvara, a Bodhisatta. The remains of Dalai Lamas are enshrined in Stupas at Lhasa.

From the 15th century onwards, architecture in Tibet took a new turn. Scores of extensive monasteries were built. And, in the 17th century the Palace of the Dalai Lama, called Potala or the Red Palace, having some 10,000 chambers was built. Mention needs also here be made of the Golden Temple at Gyan-tse, some 100 feet high. It is an interesting piece of architecture in Tibet: built in five stepped terraces used for circumambulations and surmounted by a circular drum, which in turn is crowned with a square box, a thirteen-ringed spire and a canopy in succession, the temple has numerous shrines to the Buddhas of different ages (Fig. *107*).

There are met with lovely Buddhist stupas in Tibet, known as Chortens. These, enshrining the relics, are found all over the country, specially near monasteries. These and also the tombs of grand Lamas in the Potala Palace are objects of reverential worship in Tibet. A look at a Chorten (Fig. *106*) brings into view a noteworthy feature in connection with this piece of architecture. That is that its body bears remarkable similarity to the *Bhū Bhurā*: at Pagan (Fig. *17*)

The history of Tibet is very much interwoven with the history of Nepal. Buddhism helped Tibet and Nepal to come nearer each other. In the 8th and 9th centuries strong ties of religious and cultural friendship appear to have developed between these two countries.[34]

In the field of architecture, from times immemorial natural caves in the Himalayan range were the favourite abode of hermits. This custom survives todate in Nepal and Tibet, as also in other parts of the Himalayas. Some of these caves are with religious traditions going back to the Epic and Upanishadic periods of the Indian history. Of course, these caves were mostly for residential purposes, with nothing of the shrine type of architecture in them, as found in the Buddhist rock-architecture of India.

The religious arts of Nepal and Tibet are inter-connected, so much so

33. Fergusson: *History I*, 293-4.
34. Bapat: *Buddhism*, 83.

that the Nepalese stupa is not very different from the Tibetan. Both obviously, came within the compass of the Eastern School which flourished in the adjacent country of Bihar under the Pala and Sena dynasties in Bengal from the 8th to the 12th centuries. However, there are several stupas in Nepal some quite old. Most of these are tumuli-like chaityas of moderate height, with chattravali or spire nine to thirteen tiered.

> (Also), Buddhist monasteries ... were being founded in the central valley of Nepal at the very latest from the fifth century A.D. onwards.[35]

Looking back further, we find one of the oldest stupas in the Buddhist world at Piprahwa at the Nepal border: this is said to be from the time of the passing away of the Buddha. Swayambunath and the Bodhnath (Fig. *108*) are the two among the other ancient stupas in Nepal. Certainly, these were there in their basic form when the Pagan Dynasty was ruling Burma. In shape they are a tumulus over a square base and have a box-like structure called harmika on the top crowned with a conical finial of unusual design. The special feature is the pair of huge human eyes embossed on each face of the harmika, in metal and ivory. These, looking in all four directions, make one recall the hugh faces in stone at Bayon at Angkor Thom in Cambodia, looking in all the four directions, spelling the divine omniscience. Brown, while discussing on the device of eyes attributed by some to an aspect of sun-worship as seen in the suraj-mukh or sun-face of Indian Temples, opines that

> More probably the eyes looking so searchingly into space are an outward sign of the "All seeing one."[36]

Certainly, Buddhism in Nepal is terribly mixed up with Hinduism, as evidenced by

> a four-faced lingam of Śiva, with a corresponding emblem with four Buddhas.[37]

The Temple of Maha-Buddha at Patan is an excellent example of how this sort of confusion between Hinduism and Buddhism came to be finally settled. Herein the Buddha occupies the basal floor, the Bodhisatta Amitābha the next, a small chaitya the third, a relic shrine the fourth and the apex is a jewelled-headed Vajra-dhātu. This temple of the 16th century gives an idea of the Tibetan evolution of the Buddhist architecture going on to a stage wherein the Theravāda, the Mahāyāna, and the Vajrayāna came to co-exist. This admirably reflects the evolution of the Buddhist thought in Bengal from the 8th to the 12th centuries. The

---

35. Wheeler: *Splendours*, 166.
36. Brown: *Architecture*, 197.
37. Fergusson: *History I*, 279.

new ideas from there enduringly influenced the Buddhist iconography and architecture in Tibet and Nepal. In this connection, the Temple of Bhawāni at Bhatgaon in Nepal, built in 1703 A.D., provides an excellent example. Enshrining a Tantric Goddess, it is a unique specimen of architecture: standing on a five-terraced base, it itself is five-storeyed, each storey with a sloping roof successively diminishing in width (Fig. *110*).

It was mainly through Korea that Buddhism and the ideas connected with Buddhist architecture reached Japan from China. Korea started getting its Buddhism from China as early as the 4th century: however, notwithstanding the fact of royal patronage, there were no notable developments in Buddhist doctrines or practices in Korea. All the same, as observed by Takasaki:

> Korean Buddhism was at the height of its power in the 11th century A.D.[38]

Then only Buddhism, hitherto the religion of the artistocracy, became the faith of the common people. Nevertheless, shortly Zen Buddhism entered the picture, and it continued together with a belief in Amitābha Bodhisatta. Of course, the Buddhism of Korea and Japan, as of China, is of the Mahāyāna type, which though basically one with the teachings of the Buddha, is a marked deviation from these in certain practices and beliefs.

Though Buddhism reached Japan in the mid-sixth century from Korea, it took time for it to become the religion of the masses. The ancient faith of Japan, i.e., Shintoism, had but to reconcile with the new faith through the growth of a number of national sects. A substantial nationalization of Buddhism, however, came about in the 8th and 9th centuries. Then stress came to be laid on the fulfilment of the religious life in this world besides the spiritual salvation.

The later Heian Period or the Fujiwara Period (A.D. 894-1185) when the capital shifted from Nara to Kyoto, and particularly the Kamakura Period (A.D. 1186-1333), with Kamakura as the centre, found Buddhism completely absorbed by Japan. This is a period which more or less coincides with the Pagan Period in Burma. However, while the Theravāda Buddhism was being popularized in Burma, the Mahāyāna in its Zen and other forms was catching the imagination of the Japanese nation.

Stupas in the sense of solid pagodas are rare in Japan, as also in Korea. In both these countries hollow or roomed temples are the rule. These in Japan,

---

38. Bapat: *Buddhism*, 69.

even down to the present day, are all built in timber as being better able to resist the shock of earthquakes, and may be looked upon, therefore, as the survivals of those which formerly existed in Korea, in which country they are now however in stone or brick.[39]

It is really very interesting to study the temple architecture in Japan, where the old forms of architecture continued to be favoured for a considerable period. While a temple of the Asuka Period (A.D. 552-645) is quite imposing, the temple at Nara of the early Nara Period, dated A.D. 698 [Fig. *111 (3)*], appears an improvement in the way of its artistic impression, with multi-storeyed roofs which add beauty to the structure. Simplification followed in the Late Nara period as shown by a temple named Yume-dono of A.D. 739 [Fig. *111 (4)*], which is the oldest octagonal building in Japan: it is a dainty small structure standing on a double stone terrace, with flights of steps from all the four sides. The Kasuga-Jinsha shrine at Nara was founded in the 8th century A.D. by Fujiwara families [Fig. *112 (1)*]. Here the Buddhist architecture crept into the Shinto shrine. By the early Heian Period (A.D. 794-893), some multiple storeyed temples reappeared, a tendency which continued into the late Heian Period: examples of such structures are to be found at Nara as well as at Kyoto [Fig. *112 (3)*]. However, single or double storeyed structures continued to be patronized as exemplified by a temple in the Kyoto Province of the mid-11th century: the notable feature of this temple is an elegant stupa in front of it in the open [Fig. *112 (2)*]. Another example is of a temple in the Hiroshima province, built in A.D. 1167 in the Late Heian Period [Fig. *112 (5)*]: this, however, was reconstructed in the Kamakura Period (A.D. 1186-1333), when art assumed realistic forms. The Kamakura art is exemplified by a Chapel, the Fudo-in Chapel on Mt. Koya, built in A.D. 1197 in Fujiwara style [Fig. *112 (4)*], and a temple in Shingha Province, built during the middle of the Kamakura Period [Fig. *111 (1)*]. Also, in Kamakura there remains an excellent example of Kamakura architecture of the Zen Buddhists. It is the Shari-den hall built in the Engaku-ji monastery in A.D. 1282 [Fig. *111 (5)*] "to enshrine the Buddha's tooth brought over from China"[40] Here mention may also be made of the Gateway to the Todai-ji temple built during the Kamakura Period at Nara, which exemplifies the artistic excellence and the architectural beauty of the time [Fig. *111 (6)*]. Multistoreyed temples more or less continued in later periods though markedly modified in different ways. Also, mention may here be made of the Myogongyi Temple, constructed in the 16th century, to enshrine two

39. Fergusson: *History*, 487.
40. *ABC of Japanese Art*, Board of Tourist Industry, 1937, 50.

images brought from China in the 13th century. A noteworthy feature of this temple is a tall six-storeyed solid stupa in the open, each storey being topped with a wide projection running around, the entire structure being crowned with a corbelled rod-like spire (Fig. *109*). While the design of this structure accords with the design of the earlier hollow temples, it is unique in the way that the design here is used for a solid stupa.

Part III
A Look Eastwards and Southwards

We have already looked into the developments in the temple architecture mostly contemporaneous with the Pagan Period, in India and Ceylon and have, besides, cast a look in this connection at the Himalayan and trans-Himalayan zones. Now it would be worthwhile to see eastwards and southwards of Burma. (Fig. *2*).

The religious architecture is met with in a very impressive form in what may conveniently be termed the Eastern peninsula, i.e. the entire piece of land hedged between India and China, a piece of land of which Burma forms the westernmost section. James Fergusson[41] states that the Eastern peninsula was divided into six regions namely (1) Yavana-deśa (Yonaka) in the north-east including much of the Laos districts, (2) Champa-deśa corresponding to Annam, (3) Syam-deśa in the north-west, including a part of north-eastern Burma and northern Siam, (4) Kambuja-deśa, including Cambodia, Lower Cochin China and Southern Siam, (5) Ramañña-deśa comprising of Pegu and Tenasserim and (6) Malaya-deśa meaning Malay Peninsula. This region termed Eastern Peninsula forms a part of what is termed the East Indies, which includes

> Burma, Thailand (or Siam), French Indo-China, Malaya, Netherlands Indies, and the Philippine Islands.[42]

The Netherlands Indies is now called Indonesia while the former French Indo-China is now made up of Cambodia, Laos and Vietnam. This entire region is of great architectural interest from our point of view.

We begin with Siam now known as Thailand. The architecture of Thailand may be divided into three broad periods namely: (1) Mon-Indian or Dvaravati period, up to the 10th century A.D., (2) the Khmer Period, 10th-13th century A.D., when much of the country came under the influence of the adjacent empire of Cambodia and (3) the Thai or National Period, from the 13th century onwards. Of these, the Khmer period, obviously, more or less parallels chronologically with the Pagan Period of Burmese history. But truly speaking, this is a period not at all Thai because Thais entered the picture only from about the middle of the

41. Fergusson: *History* II, 373.
42. *The New Illustrated Atlas:* London, Odham Press, Ltd., 1944, 102.

13th century when they established their capital at Sukhothai. Otherwise, as mentioned above, the country from the 10th-13th centuries was but a province of the Cambodian Empire and populated mostly by the Mons. Of course, in another century, the Thais, successful in their wars with the Cambodians, became masters of the land: they came down to have Ayuthia as their glorious capital and thence moved to Bangkok, the modern metropolis, three centuries later.

A monastry in Thailand is popularly known as the Vat (Wat). The most important building in the Vat, according to Fergusson is the Bot i.e., the sacred Temple.

> The principal feature in the Bot... (is) the great altar carrying a gilded statue of Buddha.[43]

In its rear is the pra of which there are two kinds, namely the Pra-*Cetī* and the Pra-Prang (Fig. *115*). The Pra-*Cetī* having some relics is with a solid structure with no interior compartments and is circular in plan. Its bell-shaped section corresponds to the dome of the ancient stupas in India. However, this terminates into a tapering finial. Most of the vats have only one *cetī* called the Pra *Dhātu Cetī*. That is why the vat with such a monument is known as the Wat Pra *Mahā Dhātu*. A royal city is never without a Wat Pra *Mahā dhātu*. The Pra-Prang, a tower-like structure, is a type peculiar to Siam. There are two kinds of prangs, namely (1) the one which is a prang entirely (Fig. *114*) and (2) the other with a prang on the top (Fig. *121*). Regarding the second type:

> about half-way up is the cell, with its entrance door on the eastern side, access to which... (is) obtained by a steep flight of steps, and (there are) recessed niches on the three...sides.[44]

Of the same tall imposing shape as **the Pra-*Cetī*, the** Pra-Prang instead of the tapering finial, terminates in a sikhara-like structure. Mention needs be made that the Pra-Prang is not to be confused with Bot, the latter being a conventional temple with a large image of the Buddha and the former being also with one or more images but with a structure somewhat tower-like.

In the sphere of architecture, at Dvaravati, very little remains except some fragments of building foundations. However, we can have some idea of the types of stupas there from the stone models and bas-reliefs in the National Museum at Bangkok (Fig. *113*). While in this fig. the first specimen is bell-shaped, others have more or less pot-shaped dome with ringed or multi-tiered parasol, crowned with the finial.

The majestic Pra Pathom *Cetī* at Nakorn Pathom, in Thailand, in its original form was, it seems, dome-like, with a prang added later, as

43. Fergusson: *History* II, 407.
44. Fergusson: *History* II, 407.

shown in the replica of it situated south of the main structure (Fig. *118*). This *Cetī* is reputed to be the oldest in Thailand. The old structure was completely covered by the present big *cetī* in the reign of king Mongkut, in A.D. 1853 (Fig. *117*).

The period of Khmer supremacy in Thailand (10th-13th centuries A.D.), coincides with the Angkorian Period of Cambodia. While the Mon art at Dvaravati reflected the Theravāda values, the art in Cambodia was mostly under Hindu or Mahāyāna influences.

> (During this period (i.e.,the Khmer Period), though we witness) a provincial phase of the Khmer style, as this flourished at Angkor, nonetheless the buildings of this period in Siam display in their character a certain independence of treatment significant of their historical background and earlier traditions.[45]

This spirit of independence is traceable to the traditions of earlier period and also to the Mon influence from Southern Burma. The Khmer influence is perceptible in the Lopburi school of Art which flourished from the 11th-15th centuries. An example of this is found in the Mahāyāna Buddhist temple of Pimai, built in the early 12th century, a little before Angkor Vat. Herein, there is the sanctuary tower with nagas and divinities adorning it [Fig. *120(3)*]. And, out of the two principal buildings at Lopburi having Cambodian influences, the temple of Wat Mahādhātu (Fig. *119*) c. 12th century, is the most distinctive.

> Although the architectural treatment combines elements recalling both the Indo-Aryan and Khmer styles, it is no slavish copy of either of these modes, but a definitely original effort.[46].

This temple except for the porches and that it is smaller, reminds one of the great *Bobokrī: cetī* at *Śrī Kṣetra* (Burma) (Fig. *5*). The other temple with Khmer influence at Lopburi is that of Pra Prang Sam Yot, built towards the end of the Khmer supremacy in Thailand. This temple consists of three separate shrines, with corridors between them and each surmounted by a tower [Fig. *120 (2)*]

> It displays certain elements, which associate it not with the prevailing Buddhism but with the Brahmanical faith.[47]

Another temple meriting mention is that of Wat Kukuta, also called Wat Chama Tevi, near Lampun. It assumed its present form in A.D. 1218. A pyramidal five-storeyed stupa, it is with three niches on each face of each storey for the standing images of the Buddha, thus there being 60 niches in all. There are miniature stupas at the corners of four of the five storeys. The summit stupa and the spire are missing [Fig. *120 (1)*].

45. Brown: *Architecture*, 227.
46. Brown: *Architecture*, 227.
47. Brown :*Architecture*, 228.

Later, the art assumed Thai style as illustrated by the bronze reliquary of the 13th-14th centuries, which supported by lion heads is surmounted by a stupa of the Singhalese form [Fig. *120 (5)*]. Of the numerous types of stupas at Sukhothai, the one standing on a base supported by masonry elephants is reminiscent of the Singhalese stupas [Fig. *120(4)*]. The Prang of the Great Relic Monastery, Svargaloka at Sukhothai, is a Thai adaptation of the Khmer tower [Fig. *120(6)*]. The *Cetī* Si Liem near Cheingmai, dated A.D. 1276, is architecturally peculiar in that it is square with a sitting Buddha lodged in each face at the bottom, above which there are five tiers with three standing Buddhas on each side of each storey (Fig. *116*). Its appearance reminds us of Wat Kukuta of A.D. 1218, of which it might be an imitation.

In the Ayuthian Period, art assumed more robust and independent forms. The ruins of the temple of Sri Sanphet (Fig. *122*) at Ayuthia

> (shows) that in the 15th century, in spite of indications of an approaching decadence, it was a notable work of architecture.[48]

The structure of Prang, in due course, underwent certain developments, the latest of which is seen in the *cetī* of Wat Arun, the Temple of Dawn, of the Bangkok Period (Fig. *121*).

In the course of our study of the Buddhist architecture in Siam, we found that though in the earlier period the Theravāda Buddhism flourished in the Dvaravati kingdom in the south and also in the north in the Mon settlement around Lampun and among the Lann Thai group, the Cambodian overlords of Siam with their capital at Angkor, professed the Mahāyāna faith as such or considerably mixed up with Hinduism, to which they were initially attached. However, finally the Theravāda became the religion of Cambodia.

> The modern Buddhism of Camboja is simply Siamese Buddhism which filtered into the country from about A.D. 1250 onwards.[49]

Brown classifies the Cambodian art into the Pre-historic Phase (upto A.D. 500), the Primitive Phase (A.D. 500-800), the Formative Phase (A.D. 800-1000) and the Classical Phase (A.D. 1000-1200), after which there was decline. The Formative Period is exemplified by temples such as the Mebon, Pre-Rup (Fig. *128*) and Banteay Srei, dated A.D. 969.

> The temple of Banteay Srei formerly named Isvarapura, consists of an assembly of several buildings (among which were)...three shrines or sanctuaries.[50]

An idea is had of the towers of the above temple from Figure *129*, which shows the south sanctuary. This temple is hailed as "a veritable jewel in

48. Brown: *Architecture*, 229.
49. Eliot, Charles: *Hinduism and Buddhism I*. (London, Edward Arnold and Co., 1921), xxv.
50. Brown: *Architecture*, 220.

stone."[51] Its special interest lies because of it marking the transition between the formative and the classical phases of the Cambodian architecture.

The Classical Phase starts with Śuryavarman I, who ruling for nearly the first half of the 11th century, laid the foundations of the Khmer building art. During his reign, the city of Angkor Thom was planned and the Royal Palace was built. The establishment of this imperial seat was in itself a notable achievement. The 12th century found itself engaged in marked constructional activity and several important buildings were constructed, of which one edifice is of monumental character, namely the great temple of Angkor Vat. King Śuryavarman II (A.D. 1112-1151) started its construction, and it was completed during the reign of Dharaṇīndravarman II (A.D. 1152-81). Angkor Vat, meaning 'the City Temple', was originally dedicated to the Hindu God Vishnu. However, later, under Jayavarman VII (A.D. 1181-1201), the last of the great Cambodian rulers, the Angkor Vat became a Buddhist shrine.

The Angkor Vat, located a mile south of Angkor Thom, verily is a marvel in architecture (Figs. *123, 124*). The immense stone platform over 3000 feet square, had a wide moat around it. There are pillared halls with cella for the deity and corridors after corridors of picturesque excellence (Fig. *125*). The monumental structure has super-imposed diminishing terraces, three in number, with a sikhara at each corner. In the centre of the third terrace stands the main Temple rising high into a towering turretted mass, the total height of the magnificent structure from the ground level to the pinnacle of the Temple being 210 feet. This architectural masterpiece of the Khmer art, symmetrical in form, with originality in conception, wonder-inspiring in its facade and monumental in its impression needs be seen to be understood, for according to those, including my father, who visited the place in 1961, no description or photographic representation can be a substitute for a visit to the place.

The Angkor art, sadly enough, entered its flamboyant phase by the end of the 12th century, when the ruler Jayavarman VII became imbued with the idea of grandiose elaborations. Consequently, we meet complicated patterns loaded with ornamentation at the capital city of Angkor Thom. There we find an imposing causeway, super-human figures of gods, demons and nagas and other fantastic details. The Gate of Victory there is itself a piece of ornamentation, and the towering Temple of Bayon has bas reliefs highly intricate in detail (Fig. *127*).

The Bayon Temple at Angkor Thom covers an area 500 feet square. *In the centre of this space stands the main temple rising* up in two storeys

51. *A Preface to Angkor*, (National Tourist Office of Cambodia, 1960), 8.

to 130 feet. The intricate disposition of its parts, the pyramidal mass of elevation, the processional galleries concentrically arranged with the tower in the centre having the sacred image, and the fifty towers around, which have on each of their four sides a gigantic smiling human face (Fig. *126*), making the total of 200 such faces, make Bayon a distinguished piece of architecture. Unfortunately, this grandeur of the 12th-13th centuries in Cambodia, was the last flicker in the light of Khmer architecture. For, shortly the decline set in. And, by the time of the middle of the 15th century, the strained relations with Thailand had reached their climax. The result was that in A.D. 1431 the capital at Angkor was dispoiled at the hands of the Thais.[52] This gave to the Khmer art a staggering blow, from which it never recovered.

The Cambodian empire, after the sack of its capital at Angkor, fragmented. However, the dismemberment did not spell an utter cessation of architectural activity. The different parts into which the empire broke up continued with the building activity in accord with their national genius. While Figure *137* is symbolic of this activity in Cambodia proper, Figure *134* eloquently represents the architectural genius of Laos.

In our comparative study of the *cetī* architecture in Pagan and the Buddhist architectural developments in the neighbouring countries at the time on the mainland of Asia, we feel impressed by the basic features of the impulse that actuated and guided these developments.

> It was the galloping wave of dynamic Buddhism... which had the stamina of an intellectual invincibility behind it, an all-embracing call of love as its beacon-crest and the rushing foam of human service as its vanguard.[53]

that opened a new epoch of cultural exchange in the annals of humanity, uniting East Asia as a whole into one solid cultural block. The religious architecture of this vast region, before the advent of the European or Western powers into this zone, amply testifies to this fact.

Moving out from the Asian mainland into the near Pacific, the massive proportions of the towering giganticness of the Borobudur shrine in Java attracts our immediate attention. This reminds us of the dynasty of Sailendras, which is a great name in the history of maritime empires. Established originally as a kingdom at Śrivijaya (i.e., the island of Sumatra in the immediate neighbourhood of the island of Java), the Sailendras conquered the neighbouring islands extending their power even to the Malay Peninsula in the 8th century A.D. Thence onward, they retained the mastery of the surrounding seas for over five centuries.

52. Hall, D.G.E.: *A History of South-East Asia*, (New York, St. Martins Press, 1964), 123.
53. Soni, R.L.: *The Cultural Background of India*, (Mandalay, The Institute of Buddhist Culture., 1953), 9.

Chinese accounts of the 12th century attest the fact that the Sailendras controlled the maritime traffic through the Straits.[54] The Sailendra monarchs were Buddhists professing the Mahāyāna faith which they spread to Malaysia and the other islands in the near Pacific, and also to the coastal strips of the mainland in the neighbourhood.

There is in ancient Malaysia evidence of Pallava architecture in the temples, as also of the Borobudur plan on a smaller scale. Influences of Pala architecture from India and of the Dvaravati style from Siam were also at work. An image of the Pala style found there has received the highest praise from Coedes,[55] the doyen of historians on South-East Asia.

All through the Pagan Period in Burma, the Borobudur monument was there in Indonesia along with a number of quite large and well-built Hindu complex of shrines scattered over the country. Built about the 9th century, this, rightly acclaimed as the eighth wonder of the world, represents the Golden Age of Indonesian architecture. Of course, earlier i.e., A.D. 625-750, there was building activity in Java, but mostly in honour of the Hindu God Viṣṇu. Besides, there were Buddhist temples such as Kalasan (c.778), the temple dedicated to the Goddess Tārā and planned in the shape of a Greek Cross, and also temples such as Sari A.D. 800 and Mendut—c. A.D. 800, under the Sailendra patronage. These shrines constitute the satellites of the great structure of the Borobudur, which virtually belongs to the same period.

Certainly Borobudur is a marvel. It is Indonesia's greatest cultural historical monument. In its general form a stepped pyramid raised on a hill, it consists of six quadrangular and three circular terraces, with the entire structure crowned with a big stupa. The walls of the quadrangular terraces have narrative bas-reliefs running into a total of about three miles, detailing the story of man's sojourn in the world. The circular terraces representing existences in the higher planes have seventy-two latticed stupas with Buddha images in each. The big stupa on the top has a commanding view (Fig. *133*). The entire monument contains stone statues of Buddha to a total of 505. This immense stupa some 500 feet: square and 116 feet in height, has steep flight of steps and carved arched doorways. (Fig. *132*). It certainly must have taken many years to complete: "a total of at least Seventy Five years"[56] says Brown.

The very name Borobudur is subject to different interpretations. While some interpret it as meaning 'Many Buddhas' on account of the

54. Panikkar, K.M.: *A Survey of Indian History*, (Bombay, National Information and Publications Ltd. 1947), 119.

55. Sarkar, B.H.: "Some Aspects of the Indianization of Ancient Malaya and the Role of the Brahmanas in it," *JAS*, VIII, i, 1966, 12.

56. Brown: *Architecture*, 235.

"innumerable images distributed over its various surfaces,"[57] others say:

> The word Borobudur consists of two words, 'boro' coming from the Sanskrit word 'bihara' or 'wihara' which means monastery, and the word 'budur' which is an Indonesian word meaning 'small hill'. As such Borobudur means 'monastery on a small hill'.[58]

This unique architecture, observes Brown,

> moved one writer to state that the architect's conception was to erect a stupa on a pyramid. Another... (G. Coedes) has described it as... a cupola half rising from the earth, and holding within its bosom a stepped pyramid, loaded with images.[59].

A remarkable feature of the Borobudur architecture is its spiritual significance. The journey from the base to the summit of the Borobudur, represents a pilgrimage: the pilgrim enters at the lowest level the world of sense pleasures with **Māra** at the gateway. The climbing up from terrace to terrace is symbolic of one's journey from lower states of existence to the higher.

> The lower galleries are square, this being the symbol of conditional existence while the ones on the summit are circular terraces, the circle symbolising (a move towards) the unconditioned. So the journey is from the conditioned realms... to the unconditioned **Nibbāna.**[60]

This is what is evident from the architectural design of the monument, though it cannot be said with certainty as to what actually was in the mind of the architect.

It seems, after Borobudur, building activity slagged down, as nothing better than Borobudur could be set up even though the Hindu revivalists from A.D. 860 did their best to rival Borobudur as evidenced by their complex of 150 shrines known as the Prambanam (completed A.D. 900), and other structures of the 13th-14th centuries. The Singasari temple dated A.D. 1250

> consists of a central shrine surmounted by a tall tower and having a supplementary shrine to a smaller scale projecting from each of its four sides.[61]

Other examples are the Hindu temple of Kidal, dated A.D. 1250 and the Buddhist temple of Jago dated A.D. 1268. The Majapahit period (A.D. 1294-1478), had Buddhist as well as Hindu shrines. Examples are the Buddhist shrine of Jaboeng dated A.D. 1354 and the Hindu shrines such

57. Brown: *Architecture*, 236.
58. "Tourism": *IET*, xi, June 1968, 31.
59. Brown: *Architecture*, 236.
60. De Silva, S.F.: "The Simile of the Elephant Foot Print" *VS*, 1969, 44.
61. Brown: *Architecture*, 238.

as the Papoh (A.D. 1300) and the Panataram (A.D. 1370). These only merit a passing mention. After that Islam took over the country. However, we must mention that in the Tabanar area of Bali, there were rock-cut shrines in the 11th-12th centuries. Of particular interest

> (is the) Elephant Cave,... consisting of a rock carved in the semblance of a giant elephant's head with an opening under its trunk leading to a dark cell, in some respects recalling the Tiger Cave (c. 150 B.C.) at Udaigiri, Orissa, India [62]

In fine, while the Pagan Dynasty was in power in Burma (11th-13th centuries), of all the religious monuments in the Islands of the Pacific, Borobudur (c. A.D. 850) stood head and shoulders high. It eloquently proclaimed in the objective world the height and dimensions the religious impulse soared in the mind of man at the time.

Before we close our comparative study of the temple architecture contemporaneous with the Pagan Period (11th-13th centuries), mention needs be made of the fact that the Buddhist architecture, far from remaining confined to a large part of Asia and the Pacific islands, reached as far as America as revealed by recent researches. For, at that time, there flourished a highly advanced culture and civilization in Central America. And, Chaman Lal observes:

> (that a Buddhist scene) preserved in a temple relief in Java has its parallel in the famous Pyramid Temple in... Guatemala... (also), it does have a remarkable similarity to a number of 'Life of Buddha reliefs' of the Borobudur in Java.[63]

He quotes Sir Stamford Raffles who wrote:

> The great temple of Borobudur might readily be mistaken for a Central American Temple.[64]

A Temple of 10th century Cambodia, the Baksei Chamkrong (Fig. *130*) has its identical form at Guatemala (Central America) (Fig. *131*). He mentions of a regular traffic between Asia and America in the 12th century, when there was, he asserts

> the culmination of civilization both in Cambodia and (pre-Columbian) America.[65]

As to how the contact was maintained, no less a person than Prof. Max Muller is quoted as saying that the men from Asia went to the American continent

> either across the stepping stones of the Aleutic bridge in the North or lower South by drifting with favourable winds from

62. Brown: *Architecture*, 240.
63. Chaman Lal: *Hindu America*, (Hoshiarpur, Dev Datt Shastir, 1956), 11. Hereafter this work will be referred to as Chaman Lal: *America*.
64. Chaman Lal: *America*, 13.
65. Chaman Lal: *America*, 326.

island to island.[66] (Map III).

Certainly, maritime intercourse between the two continents long before Columbus reached America, cannot be easily set aside, for even Sanchi sculptures dating back to the 2nd century B.C. testify to the use of Indian ships: moreover, an Ajanta painting has representation of a sea-going vessel and Borobudur has ships depicted in sculpture. Certainly, further research is needed to thorw more light on this subject of Asian religious influences in America at the time Pagan rulers graced the throne in Burma.

The above survey, giving a comparative view of the religious architectural developments in the neighbouring countries, contemporaneous with the Pagan Period in Burma, brings into view a fascinating scene of building activity in the annals of history. Pagan in Burma impresses us as the geographical centre of this vast series of scenes (Map IV). This magnificent panorama is found extending to India and Ceylon in the West, the Himalayas, China, Korea and Japan in the North and Thailand and Cambodia among other lands in the East. Besides, some contemporary structures of impressive grandeur adorning the islands near South-East Asia are found irresistibly calling our attention to them. A comprehensive review of the situation leads to the inevitable conviction that architecture in Eastern half of Asia at the time of the Pagan Period in Burma was mostly inspired by the impulse of religion. Though to begin with Buddhism gave the initial stimulus to this impulse, in due course Hinduism too followed suit, contributing a unique touch to the building art in the religious sphere. Moreover, Buddhism having deviated markedly in the long interval between its advent in the 5th century B.C. and the 11th-13th centuries A.D., the religious architecture found these changes well reflected in its design. Also, a significant discovery is that though the ideas for religious structures, particularly of the Buddhist and Hindu type, came from India to begin with, these came to be used in the countries abroad not slavishly but with variations in keeping with the national culture and genius. It is in the light of these observations that we can understand the facts of history to the effect that while Pagan was most engaged during the Pagan Period in raising fanes over her soil in accord with the Theravāda faith, the original teachings of the Buddha, the religious architecture took its own course in all the neighbouring countries, with marks distinctively native. Thus, while in India Indo-Aryan and Dravadian styles came into being with the sikhara and the gopuram as distinctive contributions, one or the other of which found expression in modified form in Burma, Thailand, Cambodia and other places, Ceylon popularised the harmika structure between the body

66. Chaman Lal: *America*, 307

and the spire of the *cetīs*, a structure which also found its way into some temples in the neighbouring lands. While in Tibet and Nepal, the Buddhist architecture reflected the later stages in the history of Buddhism, namely the Mahāyāna, as prevalent in Eastern India about the 8th to the 12th centuries, in China the secular architectural structure known as '*tower*' came to be used as an image house and in consequence designated a pagoda. In Japan, the Buddhist architecture took a new form, it having mostly compromised with the Shinto structures, as a result of which a distinctive architecture known by its storeyed roofs came into vogue. Nearer Burma, in the East, while Thailand developed tall pagodas termed prangs, besides the *cetīs*, Cambodia put up monumental structures at Angkor, Angkor Thom and Angkor Wat, which stood unrivalled in their grandeur, expanse and magnificence on continental Asia. Of all the structures in the near Pacific, the Borobudur in the island of Java stands head and shoulders high, proclaiming for all times the massive beauty in religious architecture, which Buddhism inspired. The magnitude of this inspiration can well be gauged by the influence it exercised across the Pacific in Central America where some Buddhist structures exactly alike to those in South-East Asia of the Pagan Period have been discovered. A survey as the above, strongly and vividly gives the impression of the sterling vitality of Buddhism, which carried with it the impulse of impressive and magnificent art across hills and dales and oceans to lands far and near, in each case expressing it in terms of the local genius, thus adequately meeting the religious needs of different climes. It indeed is an elevating idea to see that geographically the Pagan Zone stands in the heart of this vast expanse of architectural splendour.

MAP III Showing the Religious Architectural Influences across the Pacific

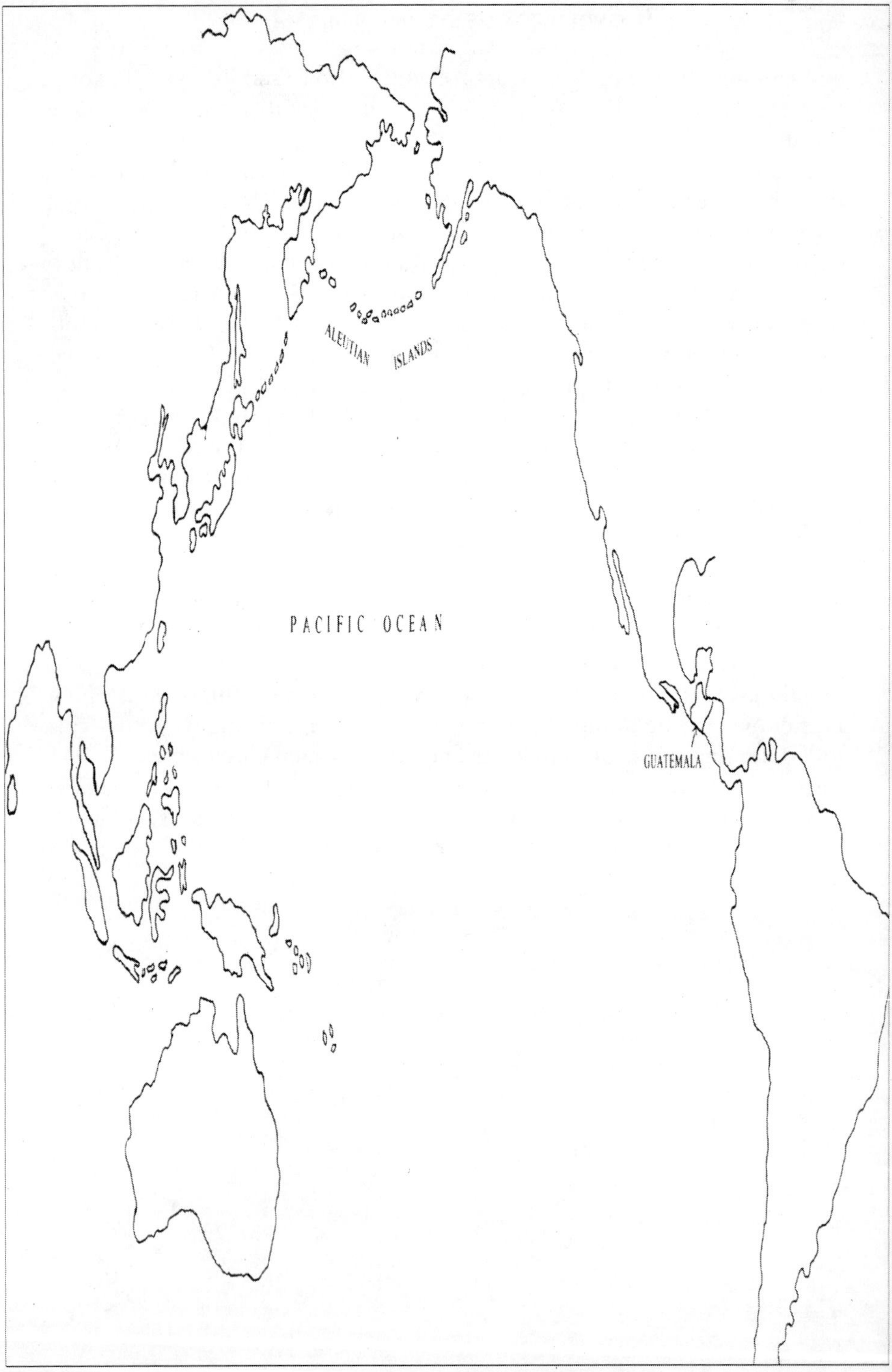

MAP IV Showing the Central Position of Pagan in relation to the Neighbouring Countries

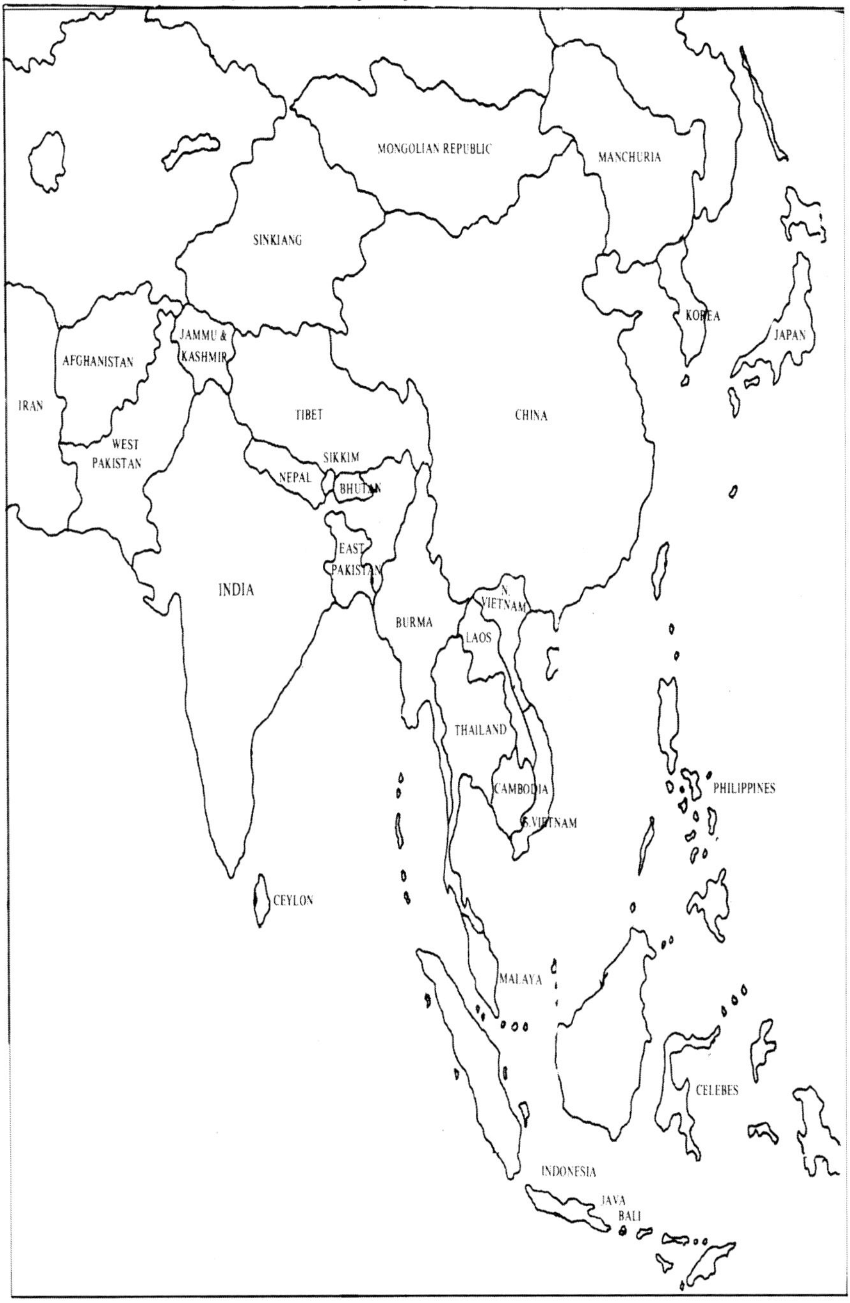

Illustrations

This section is devoted to the enumeration and explanation of the photographs of pictures and illustrations referred to in this Thesis. Most of these are from various published works and from the ASB, whereas others are original pieces. These pictures are numbered and the source of each picture is duly mentioned in terms of the abbreviations used. Also, is briefly given some requisite information of the historical background and the architectural design of the item represented. The enumeration is given in two parts, Part I devoted to the pictures from Burma and Part II dealing with pictures from the neighbouring countries.

Part I

1. *PGP,* 14-15, (1917-18):
   General view of present day Pagan from *Kanto, pallaṅ* temple.
2. *IA,* pl. XIV, between pages 16 and 17:
   Fourteen forms of stupas as found in Asia, with a descriptive note of names, date and in some cases their location attached.
3. ASB, Photo Negative No. 2818, 1926-7:
   A stone relic-chamber cover with a representation of a stupa on it: found at *Śrī Kṣetra (Mhoaujā)* in the year 1926-7. The body of the stupa closely resembles that of the Amaravati stupa in India. (Fig. 80), and also the model found at Manikyala Tope (Fig. 85). The elongated dome is surmounted by a box-like structure called 'harmika' which in turn is crowned by five successively diminishing plates called 'sattavali.' Note the five niches at the base of the dome each with a Buddha's image in *dyānqmudrā.*
4. ခေတ်ဟောင်း၊ ၄၅
   Another stone relic-chamber cover in *Śrī Kṣetra (Mhoaujā).* It is similar to the above, except that this has two plates instead of the five mentioned above.
5. ASB, Photo Negative No. 2351.1923-4:
   The *Bobokrī: cetī* at *Śrī Kṣetra (Mhoaujā)* c. 5th or 6th century A.D., as seen in the year 1923-4: it is 150 feet high—the tallest among the ancient structures in Burma. The original structures at the top are unknown, the present one being a much later construction.
6. ASB, Photo Neg. No. 421, 1906-7:

The *Bhurā:toṅ cetī:* a hollow *cetī* dated c. 5th or 6th century A.D., at *Śrī Kṣetra (Mhoaujā),* as it stood in the year 1906-7. The four corner stupas, obviously, are modern additions.

7. ASB, Photo Neg. No. 85/13703, 1967-8:
The *Koṅ:mhutoau cetī* at Sagaing, as it stood in the year 1967-8: built by king Thalun and finished after his death in 1648. According to the inscriptions it is a close copy of the *Mahācetī* in Annuradhapura (Ceylon).
8. ASB, Photo Neg. No. 7468, 1957-8:
The *Bhurā:mā cetī* at *Śrī Kṣetra (Mhoaujā)* c. 5th century A.D., as it stood in the year 1957-8. Note its cone-shaped body. The crowning structure (umbrella) at the top does not seem to be a part of the original structure.
9. ASB, Photo Neg. No. 416, 1906-7:
The Bébé temple at *Śrī Kṣetra (Mhoaujā),* c. 5th century A.D., as it stood before repairs in the year 1906-7. Its seemingly plain-shaped sikhara must not make us conclude that it was ever without ornamentations, this in view of the high accomplishments of the artists in the *Śrī Kṣetra* period.
10. ASB, Photo Neg. No. 7477, 1957-8:
The Bébé Temple as seen after repairs in the year 1957-8.
11. ASB, Photo Neg. No. 414, 1906-7:
The *Bhurā:krī: cetī* at *Śrī Kṣetra (Mhoaujā)* c. 5th century A.D., as it stood before repairs in the year 1906-7. Note its cone-shaped body which is similar to that of the *Bhurā:mā cetī* (Fig. 8). The umbrella at the top does not seem to be a part of the original structure.
12. ASB, Photo Neg. No. 94, 1903-4:
The *Ānanda* Temple (Pagan) as it stood before repairs in the year 1903-4: built by *Thiluiṅ Maṅ* in the year A.D. 1091. Said to have been built after a model at Ananta in Orissa, India. From the architectural design, it decidedly is a prince among the hollow temples at Pagan. See Fig. 16 after repairs.
13. ASB, Photo Neg. No. 7454, 1957-8:
The *Bhurā:krī: cetī* at *Śrī Kṣetra* while under repairs in the year 1957-8.
14. ASB, Photo Neg. No. 207/13825, 1967-8:
The *Bhurā:krī: cetī* at *Śrī Kṣetra* after repairs in the year 1967-8. Its original contour namely the cone-shaped body is maintained throughout. Note a slight modification on the upper part of the body, which fortunately enough does not alter the contour of the stupa.

15. SS, 1969:
Detail of the upper section of the *Ānanda* Temple, as seen after repairs in the year 1969.

16. SS 1969:
The *Ānanda* Temple after repairs, in the year 1969.

17. ASB, Photo Neg. No. 323, 1905-6:
The *Bhū Bhurā*: (Pagan) as it stood before repairs in the year 1905-6: it is an ancient structure. Its relic-casket shaped body, curving in at the base, rests on a single terrace reached by steps. Its cemented spire very well simulates the final stage of the stupas evolving out of the *kalasā* pot (Fig. 48d).

18. ASB, Photo Neg. No. 1193, 1913-14:
A ruined brick built hollow structure of circular type at Pwasaw at east of Pagan, as it stood in the year 1913-14. A circular one-room chamber which most probably had a bell-shaped body above, rests on a circular platform. It gives the hint of having been encased.

19. SS, 1969:
The *Mahābodhi* Temple (Pagan), as it stood in the year 1969: built by king *Nātoṅmyā* (A.D. 1210-34). It is a copy of the *Mahābodhi* Temple at Bodh Gaya in India (Fig. 81). A quadrangular structure tapering upwards, crowned with a spire and with niches all around having seated images of the Buddha.

20. SS, 1969:
The *Bhū Bhurā:* as seen after repairs, in the year 1969.

21. ASB, Photo Neg. No. 335, 1905-6:
The *Lokanandā cetī (Sīripaccayā)* as it stood before repairs in the year 1905-6: built by king *Anirudha* in the year A.D. 1059. Its relic-casket shaped body, curving out at the base, is surmounted by a cemented spire and rests on three octagonal terraces, having plaques for *Jātaka* stories.

22. ASB, Photo Neg. No. 225, 1904-5:
The *Cim:ñakñīama*, a Singhalese type *cetī (Sīripaccayā)* as it stood before repairs in the year 1904-5: it seems to be an 11th century structure. A richly ornamented bell-shaped body, surmounted by a box-like structure and crowned with a spire, rests on three terraces lacking any steps. Note the *cetīs* at the corners of the first and third terraces and the *kalasā* pots at the corners of the second.

23. ASB, Photo Neg. No. 13464, 1966-7:
The *Chapaṭa*, a Singhalese **Type *cetī (Ñ*oṅ-ū:)** as it stood in the year 1966-7: built by the Ven. *Chapaṭa* in A.D. 1190. The early bell-shaped body surmounted by a box-like structure, crowned with a

spire, rests on circular terraces having panels for *Jātaka* plaques.

24. ASB, Photo Neg. No. 258/13419, 1966-7:
The *Cim:ñakñīama cetī* as seen after repairs in the year 1966-7.
25. ASB, Photo Neg. No. 289/13420, 1966-7:
The *Lokanandā cetī* as seen after repairs in the year 1966-7.
26. ASB, Photo Neg. No. 300/13461, 1966-7:
The *Rhwecañ:khuṁ cetī* (*Ñoṅ*-ū:) as it stood in the year 1966-7: began by king *Aniruddha* and completed by *Thiluiṅ Maṅ* in A.D. 1090. Said to contain the sacred relics from *Śrī Kṣetra* and also those procured from Ceylon. A beautifully ornamented bell-shaped body surmounted by a cemented spire, rests on three terraces having a flight of steps in the centre of each face. The three terraces are adorned with *Jātaka* plaques and their corners have *kalasā* pots, the topmost besides having replica pagodas. The *Rhwecañ:khuṁ cetī* became the prototype of bell-shaped structures in Burma.
27. SS, 1969:
Detail of the *Rhwecañ:khuṁ cetī* showing the bell and the spire as seen in 1969.
28. SS, 1969:
The *Ṅakywainātoṅ cetī* (Pagan) as seen in the year 1969: its body architecturally speaking is a relic-casket type, curving in at the base. It is a pagoda unique in itself and its shape bespeaks its great antiquity. Most probably it was built in the pre-*Aniruddha* days. Note its upper part missing.
29. SS, 1969:
Detail of the *Rhwecañ:khuṁ cetī* showing the ornamentation on the bell and upper part of the spire.
30. SS, 1969:
Detail of the *Rhwecañ:khuṁ cetī* showing the terraces with *Jātaka* plaques and the *kalasā* pots at the corners.
31. ASB, Photo Neg. No. 251, 1904-5:
The *Rhwechaṁtoau cetī* (Pagan) as it stood before repairs in the year 1904-5: built by king *Aniruddha* shortly after his conquest of Lower Burma. An imposing structure: the early bell-shaped body, surmounted by a cemented spire, rests on five high square terraces with a flight of steps in the centre of each face. The Bell rests on two octagonal terraces. It is supposed to lodge the sacred hair relics from Pegu or Thaton.
32. ASB, Photo Neg. No. 96, 1903-4:
The *Kanto, pallaṅ* Temple (Pagan) as it stood before repairs in the year 1903-4: built by *Cañsū* II (A.D. 1174-1211). A hollow *cetī* of

impressive architecture. Architecturally a sister of the *Ānanda* and the *Sabaññu* Temples.

33. SS, 1969:
The *Rhwechaṁtoau cetī* as seen after repairs in the year 1969.

34. SS, 1969:
The *Kanto, pallaṅ* Temple as seen after repairs in the year 1969.

35. ASB, Photo Neg. No. 329, 1905-6:
The *Dhammarājika cetī* (Pwasaw—about 2 miles to the south-east of Pagan), as it stood before repairs in the year 1905-6: built by *Cañsū* II in A.D. 1198. The bell-shaped body surmounted by a cemented spire, rests on three pentagonal terraces adorned with terra-cotta *Jātaka* plaques. At the base of the *cetī*, on all the five sides are image houses containing the Buddha images.

36. ASB, Photo Neg. No. 516, 1907-8:
The *Caccanā*, a Singhalese Type *cetī (Sīripaccayā)* as it stood in the year 1907-8: built by king *Thīlui Maṅlui* (A.D. 1211-34). The early bell-shaped body surmounted by a box-like structure, crowned with a dome-shaped top, rests on four square terraces, adorned with *Jātaka* plaques and having replica *cetī* at their corners.

37. ASB, Photo Neg. No. 298/13459, 1966-7:
The *Dhammarājika cetī* as seen after repairs in 1966-7.

38. ASB, Photo Neg. No. 518/5485, 1953-4:
The *Caccanā cetī* as seen in the year 1953-4.

39. ASB, Photo Neg. No. 440, 1906-7:
The East *Phaklip*, a Singhalese type *cetī* (Sīripaccayā) as it stood before repairs in the year 1906-7: it seems to be a 10th or 11th century structure.

40. ASB, Photo Neg. No. 346, 1905-6:
The West *Phaklip*, a Singhalese type *cetī (Ṣīripaccayā)* as it stood before repairs in the year 1905-6: it seems to be a 10th or 11th century structure.

41. PGP, 62, (1953-4):
The West *Phaklip* as seen after repairs. Note the renovation at the base which incorporates 550 *Jātaka* plaques.

42. PGP, 61 (1953-4):
The East *Phaklip* as seen after repairs. Note the renovation at the base which incorporates 547 *Jātaka* plaques.

43. ASB, Photo Neg. No. 225, 13386, 1966-7:
The *Pepaṅkhyoṅ:*, a Singhalese type *cetī* (Pagan) as seen in the year 1966-7: its elongated dome resting on a low foundation indicates that it was built in the early centuries of the Pagan period.

44. ASB, Photo Neg. No. 663/11893, 1963-4:
A Singhalese type *cetī* in *Maṅ:nansū* village. The dome surmounted by a box-like structure and crowned with a spire, rests on three circular terraces having panels for *Jātaka* plaques.

45. ASB, Photo Neg. No. 1863, 1918-19:
The *Maṅgalācetī* (Pagan) as it stood in the year 1918-19: built by king *Tarukpliy* in A.D. 1284. The bell-shaped body surmounted by a cemented spire, rests on three square terraces having a flight of steps in the centre of each face. The terraces are adorned with *Jātaka* plaques and their corners have *kalasā* pots, the topmost besides having replica *cetīs*.

46. ASB, Photo Neg. No. 253, 1904-5:
The *Mraṅ:kapā cetī (Mraṅ:kapā)* as it stood in the year 1904-5: built by *Aniruddha* in the 11th century A.D. The early bell-shaped plain body surmounted by a cemented spire, resting on a single square terrace, indicates that it was built in the early centuries of the Pagan period.

47. PGP, 47, (1953-4):
The *Maṅgalācetī:*—a different view

48. HBB, 179:
A representation of stupas evolving from the *Kalasā* pot as constructed from Votive tablets of the 7th or 8th century A.D.

49. ASB, Photo Neg. No. 249/13410, 1966-7:
The *Mraṅ:kapā cetī* as seen in the year 1966-7.

50. BWS, pl. III:
On the left there are two bas-relief representations from Sanchi and Ceylon—1st century A.D., showing stupas surmounted by Chatta (umbrella) and attended to by Satti (spears), the latter bearing flags and flowers. In the middle are spears with flag and garlands fastened. It may be mentioned that Sanchi had reliefs depicting procession carrying such spears. The figures from 'a' to 'g' on the right show the evolution through which the chatta and the satti passed in the course of centuries.

51. to 54. BK:
These four *cetīs* (51 and 52 are solid *cetīs* whereas 53 and 54 are hollow temples) depict the final stage of the evolution reached during the Pagan Period so far as the end of the spire of the *cetī* was concerned. This considered together with the evolution depicted on the right side of fig. 50 gives valuable food for thought.

55. HBB, 180:
A representation of stupas evolving from the relic-casket as

constructed from votive tablets of the 6th or 7th century A.D.

56. ASB, Photo Neg. No. 95, 1903-4:
The *Sabaññu* Temple (Pagan) as it stood before repairs in the year 1903-4: built by king *Cañsū* I in A.D. 1144. It is the highest in Pagan, being 210 feet. It has five storeys: the lower two were used as residence of monks, the third for images, the fourth for library and on the fifth was constructed a *cetī*. It is thus a combination of a monastery and a shrine.

57. ASB, Photo Neg. No. 431, 1906-7:
The *Thīlui Maṅlui* Temple (Pagan) as it stood before repairs in the year 1906-7: built by king *Nātoṅmyā* in A.D. 1218. A double storeyed hollow temple surmounted by a sikhara.

58. PGP, 32, (1953-4).:
The *Sabaññu* Temple as seen after repairs.

59. PGP, 25, (1953-4).:
The *Thīlui Maṅlui* Temple as seen after repairs.

60. SS, 1969:
The *Rhwekūkrī:* Temple (Pagan) as seen in the year 1969: built by *Cañsū* I in A.D. 1131. It is an elegant temple surmounted by a sikhara crowned with a spire.

61. SS, 1969:
The *Puthuiwsāmyā* Temple (Pagan) as seen in 1969: a hollow temple surmounted by a Singhalese type *cetī*. It seems to be an early period structure: that it belongs to this period is evidenced by its dark interior lighted only by perforated stone windows, a common feature of hollow temples of the early period. Note the perforated stone windows in fig. 62.

62. SS, 1969:
The *Puthuiwsāmyā* Temple showing the perforated stone windows.

63. *PGP*, 48, (1953-4).:
The *Dhammaraṁkrī:* Temple (*Mraṅ:kapā*) built by *Īm Taw Syaṅ* (A.D. 1163-5), a hollow temple, basically cross-shaped, it in plan, is similar to the *Ānanda*, which is 210 feet square. However, unlike the *Ānanda* (Fig. 16) where vertical lines dominate giving that structure a verile look, this temple because of its horizontal lines imparts a sense of repose.

64. *PGP*, 34, (1953-4).:
The *Piṭakat-tuik* (Pagan): built by *Aniruddha* in A.D. 1058 for keeping the Buddhist scriptures. It has perforated stone windows evidencing its early date. It seems the five-tiered roof was the work of *Bhui:toaubhurā:* who repaired the monument in A.D. 1783. The

roof simulates in stone work the wooden architecture witnessed in the palaces of the later kings.

65. *PGP*, 67, (1953-4).:
The *Bhurā:sum:chū* Temple (*Maṅ:nansū*). A set of three hollow square temples connected together by corridors with paintings in the interior speaking of Mahāyānistic influences. Architecturally unique, these temples still are with a pedestal in the centre of each with the images missing. It seems to be the work of late 13th century, which is evidenced by the abandonment of a programme of further decorations in their interior.

66. ASB, Photo Neg. No. 2266, 1921-2:
Detail of the doorway to the *Kūprokṅay* Temple (*Mraṅ:kapā*) as seen in the year 1921-2: note the exquisite mouldings and the artistic touch to the frontage—the work of early 13th century.

67. ASB, Photo Neg. No. 2007, 1919-20:
Detail of the windows of the *Sabaññu* temple, showing the mouldings.

68. ASB, Photo Neg. No. 3373, 1930-1:
An encased *cetī* (*Hnatat cetī*) (*Mraṅ:kapā*) as it stood in the year 1930-1: situated close to the *Cim:ñakñīama cetī*.

69. ASB, Photo Neg. No. 2992, 1927-8:
An encased stone *cetī* (*Mhoaujā*) as it stood in the year 1927-8: found at *Toṅprañ,kun:*. Note the throne-shaped base of the *cetī*.

70. ASB, Photo Neg. No. 3390, 1930-1:
An encased *cetī* (*Sīripaccayā*) as it stood in the year 1930-1: situated to the north of *Torakyoṅ:* monastery. Note the beautifully decorated bell-shaped body surmounted by a cemented spire and resting on a throne-shaped base.

71. ASB, Photo Neg. No. 3360, 1930-1:
An encased *cetī* (*Sīripaccayā*) as it stood in the year 1930-1: situated in the middle of a field, to the north-east of *Sīripaccayā* village. Note the fully developed encased *cetī* resting on a low terrace.

72. ASB, Photo Neg. No. 3365, 1930-1:
An encased *cetī* (*Sīripaccayā*) as it stood in the year 1930-1: situated in a field to the south-east of *Sīripaccayā* village. Note the sikhara-like top of the encased *cetī* and the architectural design of the encasement which marks a departure from the orthodox style.

73. ASB, Photo Neg. No. 377, 1905-6:
An encased *cetī* (*Mraṅ:kapā*) as it stood in the year 1905-6: the encased structure evidences an evolved form while the encasement is of the shape of an early period viz., the *Lokanandā cetī* (Fig. 21)

74. ASB, Photo Neg. No. 2833, 1926-7:
Two silver stupas with eight plates called Sattavali (umbrellas), one over the other, found in *Khaṅbhakun:* (*ŚrīKṣetra*) in the year 1926-7. These have a resemblance to the structure 'h' in fig 55 representing the final form evolved out of the relic-casket. Though no monument at *Śrī Kṣetra* has yet been discovered after this form, it seems the place had *cetīs* more or less architecturally alike to this design.

75. ASB, Photo Neg. No. 365/7646, 1957-8:
The *Rhwedaguṁ cetī* (Rangoon) as seen in the year 1957-8: this *cetī* represents the finalization of the *cetī* architecture in Burma. Note its concave outline.

Note: As seen from the repairs conducted in recent years, on various monuments, it is evident that mostly the process of repair followed a scheme avoiding departure from the original form of the structure concerned. Of the very few exceptions to this common rule, the *Phaklip* (East & West) present interesting examples, for, therein the renovations at the bases are new additions.

Part II

76. AHI, 229:
The Great Stupa at Sanchi (India), known to be the earliest example of Stupa architecture, built by emperor Asoka in 250 B.C. and enlarged to double its original size a century later i.e. 150 B.C.

77. MB, Pl. XXIII, upper section:
Specimens of monolith stupas depicted as items A to E in the figure, varying in diameter from two inches to two feet found around the Mahabodhi Temple in India, put up as votive stupas by visiting pilgrims. Note the umbrella-less finial in all, the varying heights of the base, the simple harmika in A,C and D and its modified forms in B and E, also the floral decoration at the bottom and the ornamental ring around the body of E.

The same figure shows items F, G and H representing stupas as depicted in bas-reliefs: note the top of F and H ending in harmikas only whereas the top of G has a harmika crowned with a finial. Attention is also drawn to the bottom sections of the three: whereas the bottom of H is without any terrace or railing, F show a railing around the perambulatory. path and G in addition has a second terrace above.

78. *IA*, Pl. XV, between pages 16 and 17:
The Northern Gateway, the finest of the four gateways in the railing of the Sanchi stupa, built about the 1st century B.C., is a unique piece of architecture, it being historically informative and artistically

interesting it has scenes not only from the last life of the Buddha but also from the legendary accounts as given in the Jātakas. Besides representations of a number of dagabas, dharma-chakra and also trees in the body of the gateway, and a couple of Triratnas and a special Dharma-chakra crowning its top, there are represented animals—horse, elephant and lion—and also human and celestial figures in different places. Though the renunciation scene shows the Prince riding the horse, nowhere is depicted the Buddha in human form.

79. *IA*, Pl. XXIV, facing page 25:
It represents a stupa in the Karle Cave in the Western Ghats, Bombay presidency (India), dated 1st century B.C. The plain dome-shaped body surmounted by a harmika, crowned with a wooden umbrella somewhat decayed rests on a two storeyed circular base each with carved railings. The cave has more or less semi-circular roof, and is with fifteen pillars on either side with richly ornamented capitals.

80. HIEA, I, 81:
The stupa at Amaravati, Madras presidency, South India as made out from a marble bas-relief, dated c. 2nd or 3rd century A.D. The richly ornamented dome is surmounted by a harmika crowned with an umbrella attended to by spears (Satti) at the end of which are fastened flags. (Fig. 50)

81. AAI, fig. A, 52:
The Mahabodhi Temple at Buddha Gaya (India) as it stands today, built by emperor Asoka. A square truncated pyramid in form crowned with an exquisite spire, it more or less retains its original shape. It needs be mentioned that extensive repairs were conducted in the 11th century under the patronage of King *Thiluiṅ Maṅ*

82. *IA*, Pl. XXXIII, between pages 36 and 37:
The stupa at Takht-I-Bahai (North Western India)—c. 2nd century A.D. A richly decorated elongated body surmounted by a harmika crowned with a six-tiered umbrella, rests on a square base having a circumambulatory path, access to which is obtained by an elegant stairway. Note the chapels at the side for votive stupas and Buddha images. It somewhat resembles the models found at *Śrī Kṣetra*, Sultanpur and Manikyala (Figs. 3, 83 & 85).

83. *HIEA*, I, 153:
Small model of a stupa found in a tope at Sultanpur near Jalalabad (North Western India)—c. 2nd century A.D. Its elongated body crowned with a six-tiered umbrella, rests on a square base. This

stupa somewhat resembles the Takht-I-Bahai stupa of fig. 82. There is also a close resemblance to the silver models of stupas at *Śrī Kṣetra* (Fig. 74)

84. *IA*, Pl. XL, fig 7, between pages 44 and 45:
Dhamek stupa at Sarnath near Banaras, i.e. Varanasi of the olden days, ascribed to the 6th century A.D. It contains no relics but is in commemoration of some important event in the life of the Buddha, some believing it to be the exact spot where He prophesied the coming of the next Buddha viz. Buddha Maitriya. An attempt at restoration took place in about the 11th century A.D. but the work was abandoned before completion as evidenced by the unfinished upper part. Architecturally it is a massive and conspicuous structure at Sarnath rising 128 feet above the plain. The lower circular part has eight projecting faces with a niche in the centre of each, for the Buddha image.

85. *HIEA*, I, 95:
Relic casket found in a tope at Manikyala—c. 1st century A.D. An elongated body with decorative bands around it surmounted by a harmika crowned with a four-tiered umbrella, rests on a throne-shaped base. Note its resemblance to Figs. 82 & 83.

86. *IA*, Pl. LXXXVII, bettween pages 88 and 89:
Types of Sikharas in Northern India together with their location and dates. Note that while the Sikharas at Aihole, Pattadakal and Jodhpur resemble to some extent the ones crowning the hollow temples in Pagan, the sikhara at Kangra with a comparatively plain strip along the middle of its sides bears a closer resemblance to the sikhara of the *Thīlui Maṅlui, Sabaññu, Kanto, pallaṅ Rhwekūkri:* and *Bhurā:sum:chū* Temples (Figs. 57, 56, 32, 60 & 65). Moreover, another noteworthy feature is that in the Pagan temples the 'amalaka' as seen at the top of the Indian sikharas is replaced by a set of four more or less mini-pyramidal structures surrounding the base of the spire.

87. *IA*, Pl. LXVII, between pages 68 and 69:
The Great **Brihadesvara Temple,** Tanjore (South India)—c. 11th century A.D. Note its elaborately decorated pyramidal sikhara.

88. *IA*, Pl. LXXIX, fig. 1, between pages 80 and 81:
The Suchendram Temple at Travancore (South India)—16th century A.D., represents a further evolution in the Hindu Temple structure complex in the way of the erection of a highly elaborate gateway known as gopuram. Also, by then there rose in

appreciation of having a temple in the middle of a tank as seen in the figure.

89. *IA*, Pl. XCVII. bet pages 100 and 101:
The Temple of Surya at Osia, Marwar (Central India)—c. 10th century A.D. Note its sikhara. which is somewhat similar to the ones' at Pa'gan crowning the hollow temples.

90. *IA*, Pl. CXXV, between pages 128 and 129:
The Kesava Temple at Somnathpur, Mysore (India), dated A.D. 1269. Note the complicated architectural design permeating through the entire structure, in contrast to the Buddhist temples at Pagan of the same period. Noteworthy is the stellate-shaped high platform in keeping with the projecting angles of the triple temple itself, with a seven feet wide space all around for circumambulation.

91. *IA*,, Pl. CXVII, bet pages 120 and 121:
The Larger Sas Bahu Temple, Gwalior (Central India), showing the main hall, belonging to the late 11th century A.D., instances another example of highly evolved but terribly complicated multi-storeyed architecture, in contrast to the hollow temple at Pagan of the same period.

92. *SA*:
Shapes of six types of Singhalese Dagabas viz. 1. bell shaped, 2. pot-shaped,- 3. bubble-shaped, 4. paddy-heap shaped, 5. a variation of 'bell-shape' with a peculiarly different top and 6. a variation of 'bubble-shape' with amalaka top.

93. *DC*:
The Kiri Vehara at Polonnaruwa (Ceylon). built by king Parakramabahu (A.D.1153-1186). Note the massive bubble-shaped mound simulating the Sanchi Tope (Fig. *76*) The box-shaped harmika crowned with a spire constitutes a characteristic of the Singhalese stupas termed Dāgabas.

94. *SA*, Pl.15:
A shrine on pillars evidencing a further evolution of the two-storeyed temple in Ceylon.

95. *IA*, Pl. CXLIX, between pages 152 and 153:
The Wata Dage or Hall of the Relic at Polonnaruwa (Ceylon): built by **Parakramabahu the Great** (A.D.1153-1186). It is a large circular temple of a notably graceful style with a high platform reached by eight steps with well executed sculptured designs all around. No comparable structure of this design is found at Pagan of the period.

96. *SA*, Pl.11:
The Lankatilaka or Jetawanarama at Polonnaruwa, (Ceylon): built by Parakramabahu I (A.D. 1153-1186). The largest hollow temple in Ceylon with a tall 60 feet image of the Buddha installed in it.

97. *AAI*, figure A, 110:
Moonstone: a semi-circular stone artistically carved with designs of animals and birds as well as floral decorations used as the first stepping stone to a flight of stairs reaching the platform of generally a temple and sometimes of an important residence. Such an item though missing in the Burmese architecture in its Singhalese shape is all the same met with in same monasteries at present in a modified form as illustrated below. Also, at *Bissaṇui:* there is found a moonstone, which, however, lacks the artistic touch so very common with the Singhalese moonstones.

97. Part II

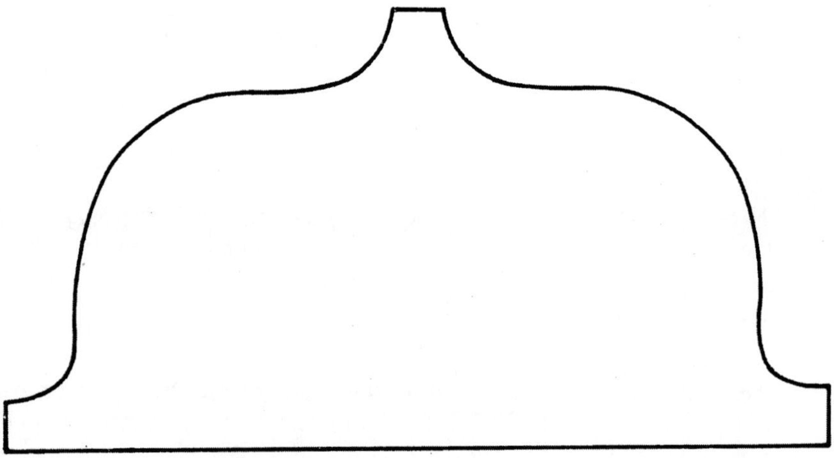

98. *HIEA*,, II 462:
The gateway with its three openings leading to the dagaba in white marble near Peking, constructed in A.D. 1780 in memory of the Teshu Lama Eradeni who died in Peking. The gateway may be regarded as the Chinese and the latest edition of the earliest gateways as seen around the Sanchi Tope in India.

99. *HIEA*, II, 465:
A Chinese grave consisting of a simple conical mound of earth: verily a *thūpa* in the etimological sense, reminding one of the period when such mounds were heaped over the graves of the dead in India before the thūpa assumed a religious significance under Buddhistic influences.

100. *HIEA*, II, facing page 459:
The Temple of Heaven or the Great Dragon, Peking (China)— A.D. 1420, evidences the developments the Chinese religious architecture underwent in later ages. It is a circular temple with three terraces and with a three-tiered roof.

101. *SE*, 25:
The Islamic minaret at Samara, Baghdad attached to a mosque, constructed by the grandson of Harun al Rashid in the 9th century A.D. It is a brick structure, 160 feet high.

102. *IA*, Pl. CLIX, between pages 160 and 161:
The octagonal pagoda at Sung Shan, Honan, (China) dated A.D. 523: it is the oldest brick building in China.

103. *HIEA*, II, page 470:
The porcelain tower, Nanking (China), commenced in A.D. 1412 and finished in A.D. 1431. It is also known as the Temple of Gratitude, it having been erected in gratitude to an empress of the Ming family. Though originally used as a treasury, an astronomical observatory or a watch tower, in due course these began to function as pagodas with images of the Buddha in the lower storey, although the above may be used as a watch tower.

104. *IAC*, facing page 145:
The Qutb Minar, Delhi (India) constructed by the Turkish ruler at Delhi in A.D. 1231-32. It is 242 feet high.

105. *IA*, Pl. CXII, fig. 1, between pages 116 and 117:
Jaina tower at Chitor, Rajasthan (India),—c. 12th century A.D. and dedicated to Adinath, the first of the Jaina saints. It is an eight storeyed structure, elaborately ornamented about 80 feet in height with an open pillared pavilon at the top.

106. *AAI*, fig. B, 99:
Chorten, the Buddhist stupa in Tibet. The body of the stupa crowned with a ringed spire, rests on a high platform. A noteworthy feature is that the body of the stupa has a remarkable similarity in form to the *Bhū Bhurā:* at Pagan (Fig. *17*)

107. *HIEA*, I, facing page 294:
The Golden circular Temple at Gyan Tse (Tibet), is a structure of its own kind. The circular drum surmounted by a small square crowned with a thirteen-ringed spire topped with a canopv, rests on five recessed terraces used for circumambulations. It is about 100 feet high.

108. *IA*, Pl. CXLII, between pages 144 and 145:
The Bodhnath Temple (Nepal), said to be dating back to a distant date. The huge dome (90 feet in diameter) surmounted by a harmika

embossed with a pair of huge human eyes on each face crowned with a stepped pyramidal brick spire, rests on three terraces. The dome seems quite an ancient structure but the spire seems to be a much later addition. Note the dome which resembles the Great Tope at Sanchi.(Fig.76).

109. *YE,* 17:
The main hall of Myogongyi Temple (Toyokawa, Japan), dated c. 16th century. In it two images brought from China in the 13th century were enshrined in A.D. 1541. Note the stupa in the foreground.

110. *IA,* Pl. CXVIII, fig. 5 between page 120 and 121:
Detail of the roof of the Bhawāni Temple at Bhatgaon (Nepal) — dated A.D. 1703, evidences the evolution the roof of the temple underwent in Nepal. It more or less bears a resemblance to the Pyatthats of later periods in Burma.

111. *JA,* fig. 68, 40:
Fig. 1
The Ishiyama-dera Taho-to Temple, Shingha province (Japan): built during the middle of the Kamakura peroid (A.D. 1186-1333). Note the double roof crowned with a ringed spire.

JA, fig.7, 4:
Fig. 2
Torii as a gateway to a shrine forms an important part of religious architecture in Japan. Known since the Archiac period, it assumed Buddhist significance when a member of it was constructed curved as shown in the figure where its upper part is curved.

JA, fig.18, 10:
Fig. 3
The Yakushi-ji To-to temple, Nara Province (Japan): built during the early Nara Period in A.D. 698. It was bodily shifted to the present capital Nara in A.D. 718. It is a graceful three-storeyed structure with a pent-roof on each storey.

JA, fig.24, 13:
Fig. 4
The Horyu-ji Yume-Dono temple, Nara Province (Japan): built during the late Nara period in A.D. 739 and reconstructed during the Kamakura period (A.D. 1186-1333). In reconstructing, the original form of the building was maintained.

JA, fig.60, 35:
Fig. 5
The Engaku-ji Shari den monastery at Kamakura, (Japan): built during the Kamakura period in A.D. 1282. It exemplifies a rare

specimen of Buddhist architecture of the Zen sect.

JA, fig. 56, 33:

Fig. 6

The gateway to Todai-ji Nandai-Mon Temple at Nara (Japan): built during the Kamakura period (A.D. 1186-1333) it exemplifies the artistic excellence and architectural beauty of the time.

112. *ABCJA*, fig. 61, between pages 54 and 55:

Fig. 1:

The Kasuga-Jinsha shrine at Nara (Japan): built in the 8th century, it is an excellent example of Shinto architecture.

JA, fig. 49, 29:

Fig. 2:

The Hokai-ji Amida-Do, Kyoto Province (Japan): built in the mid 11th century A.D. in the late Heian Period. Note the elegant stupa in the open in front of it.

SE, 245:

Fig. 3:

The Deigo-ji Pagoda, Kyoto (Japan): this elegant stupa was built during the late Heian period in A.D. 951.

ABCJA, facing page 84:

Fig. 4:

The Fudo-in Chapel the oldest building on Mount Koya, built during the Kamakura period in A.D. 1197.

JA, fig. 51, 30:

Fig. 5:

The Marodo-sha Honden of Itsukushima Jinga, Hiroshima Province (Japan): built in the late Heian period in A.D. 1167 and reconstructed in A.D. 1227-1247.

113. *AT*, 49:

Various types of Dvaravati stupas from stone models and bas reliefs in the National Museum of Bangkok. Note that the base, the body and the spire of each model represents a distinctive type: while the base in these models varies from a throne-shape to a terrace type, the body has styles varying from pots of diverse shapes to a bell form and the spire has umbrellas or ringed mouldings, depicted in their different stages of evolution, surmounted by finials tapering, ovular or rounded.

114. *HIEA*, II, 405:

A pagoda at Ayuthia of the type of pra-prang. Note its body which though comparatively short resembles the *Bobokrī:* at *Śrī Kṣetra* (Burma) in form. (Fig. 5)

115. *HIEA*, facing page 407:
The Pra-cetī enshrining the sacred relics having near it the pra-prang enshrining the image of the Buddha. Note in Thailand these two structures obviously are distinguished from one another architecturally as well as functionally.

116. *C*, facing page 43:
The Si Liem *cetī* near Cheingmai (Thailand) dated A.D. 1276. Note its five-storeyed pyramidal-shaped body with the statues of three standing Buddhas on each side of each face.

117. *VP*, 2505-6, facing page 62:
The Pra Pathom *cetī* at Nakorn Pathom (Thailand) as seen today. Constructed in A.D. 1853 by king Mongkut to encase an original *cetī* (Fig. 118), reputed to be the oldest *cetī* in Thailand: the encased *cetī* is visible through a peep hole in the hollow encasement.

118. *PC*, facing page 6:
A replica of the original *cetī* at Pra Pathom situated to the south of the main structure.

119. *IA*, Pl. CLX, between pages 164 and 165:
The Wat Mahadatu *cetī* at Lopburi (Thailand)—c. 12th century A.D. This temple except for porches and its hollow interior reminds one of the shape of the Bobokrī:cetī at ***Śrī Kṣetra*** **(Burma) (Fig. 5).**

120. *AT*, 50:
Fig. 1
The Wat Kukuta also called Wat Chama Tevi near Lampun (Lowapura) (Thailand). The present form dating back to A.D. 1218, is a pyramidal, five-storeyed structure with niches on each side of each storey for the standing images of the Buddha.

AT, 77:
Fig. 2
The Pra Prang Sam Yot at Lampun (Thailand): built in the 13th century A.D., comprised of three separate shrines, each surmounted by a tower.

AT, 75:
Fig. 3
The Mahāyāna Buddhist Temple of Pimai, built in the early 12th century A.D., obviously an architectural novelty with nagas and divinities adorning it.

AT, 100:
Fig. 4
The elephant supported stupa, Sukhodaya (Thailand)—c. 13th century A.D. The stupa is reminiscent of the Singhalese dagabas.

AT, 78:
Fig. 5
A bronze reliquary—c. 13th century: its upper section simulates a Singhalese dagaba: note the Buddha images around the middle of the structure and the ornamented base.

AT, 101:
Fig. 6
Prang of the great relic monastery, Svargaloka (Thailand). It is a Thai imitation of a Khmer tower.

121. *VP*, 2504, facing page 29:
Wat Arun or the Temple of Dawn, Dhanpuri (Thailand)—18th century A.D. Note the number of terraces leading up.

122. *RMTS*, facing page 11:
Wat Pra Srisanphet, Ayuthia (Thailand), a 15th century A.D. structure. Note the Singhalese influence in these *cetīs*.

123. *IA*, Pl. CLV, between pages 156 and 157:
Aerial view of Angkor Vat (Cambodia), a 12th century marvel in architecture.

124. *IA*, Pl. CLVI, facing page 160:
A conjectural restoration of the Temple of Angkor Vat (Cambodia).

125. *PA*, pages 12 and 13:
Detail of the upper section of Angkor Vat (Cambodia). Note the extensive corridors below/above which rise four towering structures at the corners, with the monumental structure in the middle: the exquisite carvings on these are noteworthy.

126. *IA*, Pl. CLVII, between pages 160 and 161:
Detail of the Tower in stone of the Temple of Bayon, Angkor Thom (Cambodia), a 12th century structure. It is one of the fifty towers at the place. The architectural design with the four sculptured smiling faces around is noteworthy.

127. *PA*, 20:
The temple of Bayon, Angkor Thom (Cambodia)—full view—c. 12th century A.D.

128. *PA*, 10:
The Pre Rup Temple Angkor (Cambodia)—c. 9th or 10th century A.D. This depicts the phase of architecture among the Khmers before it evolved to the Angkor Wat plane.

129. *IA*, Pl. CLIX, between pages 160 and 161:
Detail of the South Sanctuary of the Temple of Banteay Srei, Angkor (Cambodia): built in A.D. 967, during the reign of

Rajendravarman II. Note the rich architecture applied to the structure. It is one of the gems of Khmer architecture and depicts the transitional phase in the architectural field.

130. *PA*, facing page 6:
The Temple of Baksei Chamkrong (Cambodia): a 10th century temple resting on four high terraces having flight of steps on each face.

131. *HA*, Preceding page 1:
The structure on the left depicts the same temple as shown in fig. 130. The figure on the right is of a temple in distant Gautemala in Central America. Note the remarkable similarity in the architectural design of this with that of the temple depicted on the left in Cambodia of the 10th century A.D.

132. *IA*, Pl. CLXIV, between pages 168 and 169:
Aerial view of the monumental stupa of Borobudur, Java (Indonesia)—c. 850 A.D. Note its vast pyramidal structure with terraces leading to the top platform which is adorned with a central stupa surrounded by a number of smaller stupas arranged in concentric circles.

133. *AAI*, 183:
Detail of upper section of the Borobudur. Note the central stupa towering above the surrounding stupas.

134. *YTB*, 19:
The *Cetī* in Laos. The design, though basically a stupa at the bottom, is uniquely national in the way of its assemblage of architectural designs of harmika, spire and its top, to suit the sense of harmony and beauty in keeping with the native taste.

135. *TCM*, 60:
The temple at Bhitargaon in the Cawnpore district (North India): c. 4th century A.D., is a peculiar style of brickwork. Note the outer ornamentation of terra-cotta sculpture and the body rising in bold mouldings interspersed with decorative panels. The striking feature of this structure is that it as a whole bears comparison with the encasement in fig. 72 at Pagan.

136. *YTB*, 16:
The ancient Shrine at Nalanda (India) is significantly tower-shaped: multistoreyed, it has artistically executed pillars and projecting mouldings and also niches for images all around. It might be that some structure as this in India gave to the Chinese pilgrims the idea of using their already existing towers in China, as image houses.

137. *YTB*, 20:

An ancient *Cetī* in Cambodia: a fully evolved structure, beautifully comparable with the Pagan *cetīs* in its architectural design of the terraces, the bell and the spire and also the figures at the corners of the terraces. Though this *cetī* has all the ingredients of the fully evolved *cetīs* in Pagan, a careful comparison elicits the difference to the effect that not only the body of the cetī is comparatively elongated but also the spire is broadbased enough to give the body and the spire taken together the appearance of a cone. It might be that the architect gained his initial inspiration from the descriptions given by some visitors or skilled slaves from Pagan, as did *Thiluiṅ Maṅ* from the descriptions given by refugees from India for his *Ānanda* Temple.

138. *L*, 32:

Burial Mounds marking the graves of a poor family in China: the coffins are laid in the ground and earth pilled over them. Ref. also fig 99. This compares very well with the burial mounds in pre-Buddhist India.

Bibliography

The present work, devoted to the evolutionary phases in the *cetī* architecture relating to the Pagan Period in Burma (11th-13th centuries), is the result of a careful study of the Buddhist religious architecture going back to its earliest phases in India. As no work is yet available exclusively dealing with the subject, so far as the Pagan Period is concerned, I had but to make use of the available material scattered in a number of publications, both treatises and magazines, which have been detailed in the bibliography to this thesis. My gratitude freely flows to one and all of the authors and publishers of these, who made available a vast store of knowledge on the subject. However, without being invidious, I am with feelings of special indebtedness to certain authors in appreciation of the specific use made of their observation and views on certain aspects of the subject or for the illustrations, tables, maps or photos used from their works. Outstanding among these are G.H. Luce, James Fergusson, Percy Brown, Lu Pe Win, Dr Than Tun, Mortimer Wheeler, Benjamin Rowland, H. Sarkar, S. Watterson, Chaman Lal, P.V. Bapat, M.R. Anand, J. Sarkar, A. Cunningham, B.G. Gokhale, C.E. Godakumbura, R.L. Soni, ဝိန်မောင်ဦး နှင့် ဇေယျပဏ္ဍိတ· Most of the above material was had either from the Library of the Arts & Science University of Mandalay, and its History Dept. or through the courtesy of Dr R.L. Soni and U Aung Thaw, Director of Archaeology, Government of the Union of Burma, to whom I owe thankfulness. Also, the Archaeological Survey Burma has earned my special gratitude for a large number of photograph-prints supplied for use in this work. There are also a few photos owed to U Bo Ke of the Archaeological Department at Pagan, to whom as well I tender my thanks.

It needs, however, be mentioned that besides the publications listed in the bibliography other works had to be studied. This, in order to be duly equipped with the background knowledge of Buddhist architecture and doctrines. Without a supplementary study as this, the subject could not be grasped in the right perspective. For facilities in this direction, I am sincerely obliged to Daw Tin Hla, Librarian, the National Library, Mandalay, to the Ven. U Thawbita (Shwegaingtha), to the Ven. U Thu Wanna, and the Ven U Ponnyabiwuntha, all of the Sagaing Hills.

In the course of my studies I found that these needed to be supplemented by personal visits to Pagan, *Śrī Kṣetra* and Rangoon. This helped to understand things in their correct perspective. Also, the courtesy I was privileged to enjoy at the various libraries, particularly at the National Library Mandalay, the Arts and Science University Library, Mandalay, the Library of the Archaeological Survey Burma, the Library of the Institute of Advanced Buddhistic Studies and. the Library of the Ramakrishna Misson at Rangoon and at the Museum and Library of U Kyaing, Prome, merits mention with grateful appreciation. Besides, the personal visits paid to U Mya, a retired archaeologist of note, now past 90 years of age and to Col. Ba Shin currently compiler at the Historical Commission, Burma, proved fruitful in the way of certain information had in connection with the subject under study. While the former's experiences, among others, those connected with *Bobokrī:* at *Śrī Kṣetra* enriched my knowledge regarding its internal structure, the latter's work 'Lokahteikpan' encouraged me to look at with hope of similar works appearing at some further date on individual *cetīs* at Pagan.

I must also record my sense of gratitude to Daw Htay Kyi. She in 1965, as a lecturer in the Arts and Science University, Mandalay, prompted me to take history as my subject for the Master of Arts degree. Thus initiated, I went through majoring into the subject, of which this thesis is the fruit.

I would be failing in my duty in leaving out two, among many other names in the acknowledgement. One is that of Myanaung U Tin, a former Minister of Health in Burmese cabinet, who evinced a considerable interest in my work and whose encouragement was throughout a pillar of hope to me. Another is that of my father, **Dr R.L. Soni,** whose interest in Burmese culture and history, made him ever happy to help me in every way possible, to make me work for a good contribution on the subject, so as to help the future students to be encouraged to do research and make further contributions of valuable and lasting character on the important theme of the evolutionary process in *cetī* architecture in Burma.

This thesis is written from the study of the photographs of Pagan *cetīs* mostly supplied by the Burma Archaeology Survey Department. Books and periodicals consulted as secondary source material are as follows:

ABC of Japanese Art, (Board of Tourist Industry, 1937).

Amended List of Ancient Monuments in Burma, (Rangoon, Supdt. Govt. Printing and Staty., Union of Burma, 1960).

Anand, Mulk Raj: "Seven Lamps of Indian Architecture-II", *IM*, 2nd May 1948.

Angkor, A Preface to, (National Tourist Office of Cambodia, 1960).

Atlas, The New Illustrated, (London, Odham Press, Ltd., 1944).

Aung Than: *Shwedagon,* (Rangoon, Hanthawaddy Press, 2nd Edn. 1957).

Aung Than Tun: "Burmese Pagodas", *GM*, XI, x, Oct. 1964, 14-19.

Bapat, P.V.: *2500 Years of Buddhism*, (Delhi, Ministry of Information and Broadcasting, Reprinted 1959).

Brown, Percy: *Indian Architecture (Buddhist & Hindu),* (Bombay Taraporevala Sons & Co. Ltd., 1942).

Chaman Lal: *Hindu America,* (Hoshiarpur, Dev Datt Shastri, 1956).

Cornforth, Maurice: *Dialectical Materialism I,* (Calcutta, National Book Agency, 1965).

Cowell, E.B.: *The Jataka III,* (London, Luzac & Co. 1957).

Cunninghan, A.: *Mahabodhi,* (Varanasi, Indological Book House, 1892).

De Silva, S.F.: "The Simile of the Elephant Footprint", *VS*, 1969, 41-44

Duroiselle, C.: *Guide to the Mandalay Palace,* (Calcutta, Government of India, Central Publication Branch, 1931).

Eliot, Charles: *Hinduism and Buddhism,* (London, Edward Arnold & Co., 1921).

Fergusson, James: *History of Indian and Eastern Architecture I & II,* (Delhi, Munshiram Manoharlal, 1967).

Godakumbura, C.E.: *Sinhalese Architecture,* (Colombo, Department of Cultural Affairs, 1963).

Gokhale, B.G.: *Buddhism and Asoka,* (Bombay, Padma Publications Ltd., 1948).

Hall, D.G.E.: *A History of South-East Asia,* (New York, St. Martins Press, 1964).

Hasan, Yakub: *Temples, Churches and Mosques,* (Madras, G.A. Natesan & Co., 1926).

Le May, Reginald: "The Cultural Background of Burma", *GM*, XI, ii, Feb. 1964, 31-5.

Luce, G.H.: "The Ancient Pyu", BRSFAP II, 1960, 307-21.

Luce, G.H.: "Pagan Architecture, A General Survey", *GM,* I, v, March 1954. 25-7.

Lu Pe Win: *Pictorial Guide to Pagan,* (Calcutta, Sree Sarawaty Press, 1955).

Lu Pe Win: "Some Aspects of Burmese Culture", *JBRS*, XLI, i & ii, Dec. 58, 19-37.

Majumdar, Raychaudhuri & Datta: *An Advanced History of India* (New York, St. Martins Press, 1965).

Mandalay and Environs, (Rangoon, Ministry of Union Culture,

Government of the Union of Burma).

Mandalay Palace; (Directorate of Archaeological Survey, Ministry of Union Culture, 1963).

Man:nansu Inscription, A.D. 1228, Pl. 73, Line 8-10.

Moledina, M.H.: *My Impressions of the Far East,* (Poona, M.H. Moledina, 1936).

Nyanaponika: *The Life of Sariputta,* (Kandy, Buddhist Publication Society, 1966).

Ozhegov, Sesrge S.: "Originality of Burmese Architecture", *F,* II.ix, Dec 7, 1963, 17-20.

Panikkar, K.M.: *A Survey of Indian History,* (Bombay, National Information & Publications, Ltd., 1947).

Rhys Davids: *Buddhist India,* (Delhi, Motilal Banarsidass, 1975).

Rhys Davids, T.W.: *Dialogues of the Buddha,* (London, Oxford University Press, 1910).

Robertson, Alec: "Full-Moon Poya Days", *WB,* XVI, ii, June 1968,.

Rowland, Benjamin: *The Art and Architecture of India,* (Harmondsworth, Penguin Books Ltd., 1954).

Sarkar, B.H.: "Some Aspects of the Indianization of Ancient Malaya and the Role of the Brahmanas in it" *JAS,* VIII, i, 1966, 1-17.

Sarkar, H.: *Studies in Early Buddhist Architecture of India,* (Delhi, Munshiram Manoharlal, 1966).

Sarkar, J.: *India Through the Ages,* (Calcutta, M.C. Sarkar & Sons Ltd., 1950).

Soni, R.L.: *The Cultural Background of India,* (Mandalay, Institute of Buddhist Culture, 1953).

Soni, R.L.: *A Cultural Study of the Burmese Era,* (Mandalay, World Institute of Buddhist Culture, 1955).

Soni, R.L.: *Notes on History* (unpublished).

Soni, R.L.: "Theri Khettaya—I & II", BRMNT, April 2nd & 9th, 1951.

Than Tun: *History of Buddhism in Burma* (Pagan Period.) (Rangoon, Peoples' Literature Publications, 1962).

Than Tun: "History of Mandalay", *AM* I, 1968-9, 197-202.

Than Tun: "Religious Buildings in Burma, A.D. 1000-1300", *JBRS,* XLII, ii Dec. 1959, 71-80.

Than Tun: "Religion in Burma", *JBRS,* XLII, ii, Dec. 1959, 47-69.

Than Tun: "Social Life in Burma, A.D. 1044-1287", *JBRS,* XLI, i & ii, Dec. 1958, 37-47.

Tin Hla Thaw: *The Development of the Buddha Image in Burma,* (M.A.

Thesis, School of Oriental & African Studies, University of London, 1963).

"Tourism", *IET*, ii, June 1969, 27-42.

Valisinha, Devapriya: *Buddhist Shrines in India*, (Colombo, The Maha Bodhi Society of Ceylon, 1948).

Watterson, J: *Architecture Five Thousand Years of Building*, (New York, W.W. Norton & Co. Inc., 1950).

Wheeler, Motimer: *Splendours of the East*, (London, Weidenfeld Nicolson Ltd., 1965).

Yule, H, & Burnell, A.C.: *Hobson-Jobson*, (Delhi, Munshiram Manoharlal, 1968).

–စိန်မောင်ဦး၊ "သရေခေတ္တရာ မြို့ဟောင်း"၊ *ပညာပဒေသာ*၊ ရန်ကုန်၊ အတွဲ ၃၊ အပိုင်း ၁၊ ဇန်နဝါရီ၊ ၁၉၆၈၊ စာမျက်နှာ ၁၆၃-၂၀၉

–ဇေယျပဏ္ဍိတ (ညောင်ရမ်း ဆရာတော်)၊ *စေတီဘုရား တည်ထားနည်းကျမ်း*၊ (ရန်ကုန်၊ ၁၃၂၅)

–ဘုရားဖြူဆရာတော်၊ *သာသန ဗဟုဿုတပ္ပကာသနီ*၊ (ရန်ကုန်၊ ၁၂၉၀)

–*ရှေးရိုး မြန်မာပန်းချီ*၊ (ရန်ကုန် ရှေးဟောင်းသုတေသနဌာနခွဲ၊ ပြည်ထောင်စု ယဉ်ကျေးမှုဌာန၊ ၁၉၆၆)

–သန်းထွန်း၊ *ခေတ်ဟောင်းမြန်မာရာဇဝင်*၊ (ရန်ကုန် မဟာဒဂုံစာပေထုတ်ဝေရေး၊ ၁၉၆၄)

INDEX

[1]

VARIOUS FORMS OF STUPA

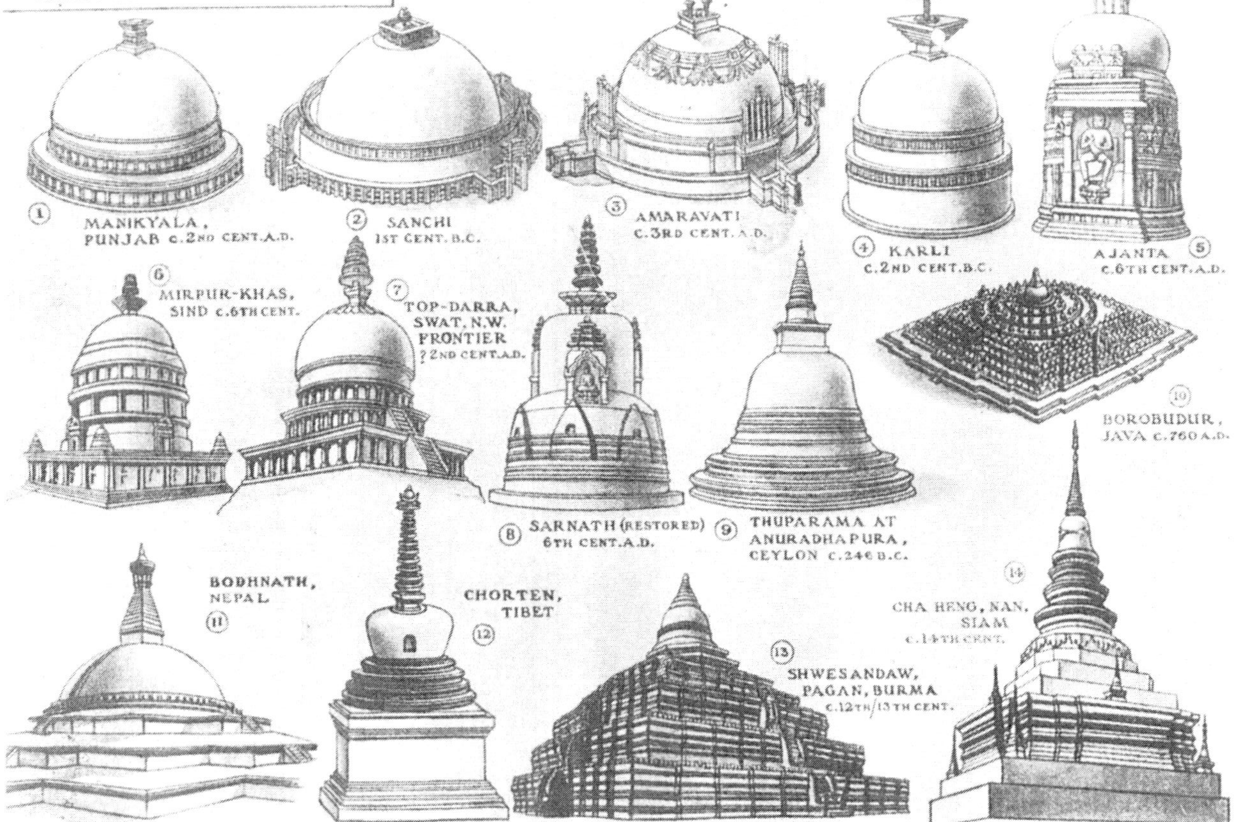

[3]

[4]

[5]

[6]

[8]

[7]

[9]

[10]

[11]

[12]

[13]

[14]

[15]

[16]

[18]

[17]

[19]

[20]

[21]

[22]

[23]

[24]

[25]

[26]

[27]

[28]

[29]

[30]

[31]

[32]

[33]

[34]

[35]

[36]

[37]

[38]

[39]

[40]

[41]

[42]

[43]

[44]

[45]

[46]

[47]

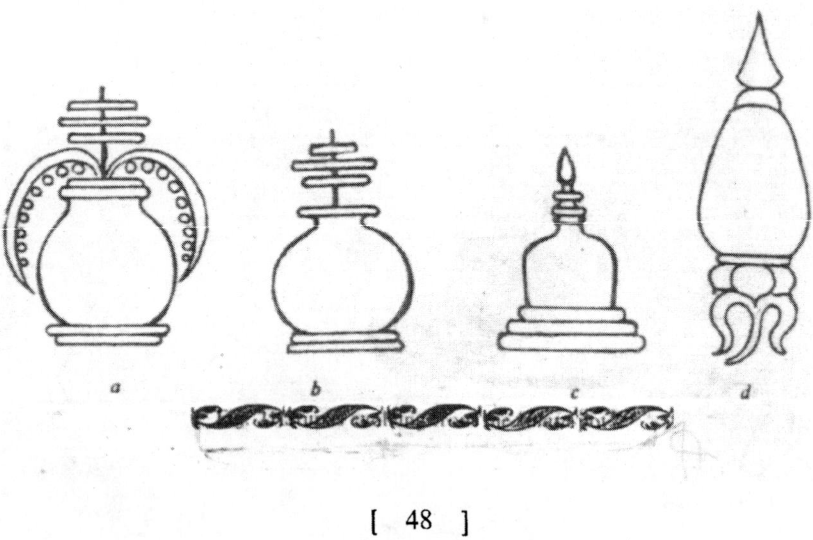

[48]

[49]

[50]

[51]

[52]

[53]

[54]

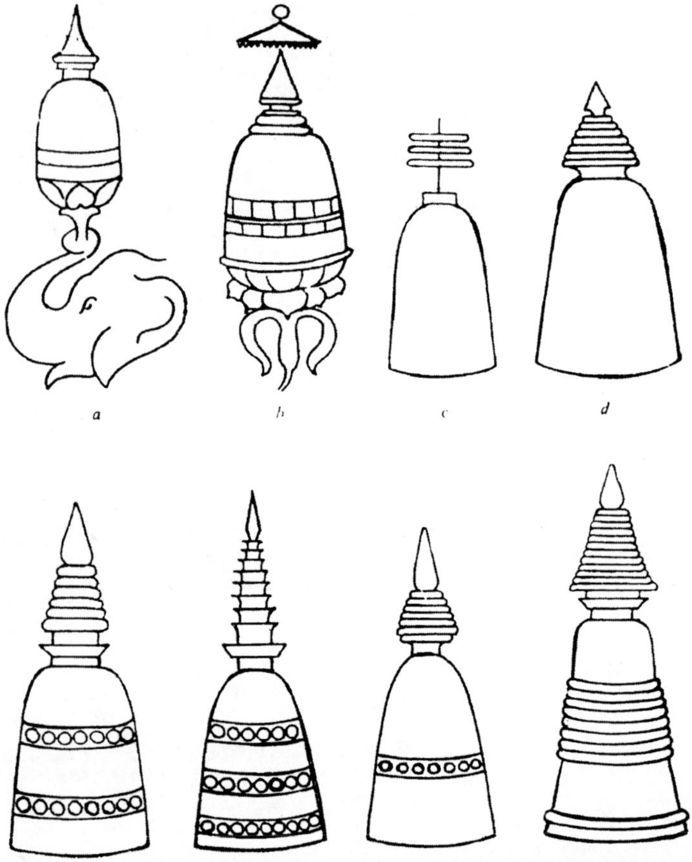

a b c d

e f g h

[56]

[57]

[58]

[59]

[60]

[61]

[62]

[63]

[64

[65]

[67]

[66]

[69]

[68]

[70]

[71]

[72]

[73]

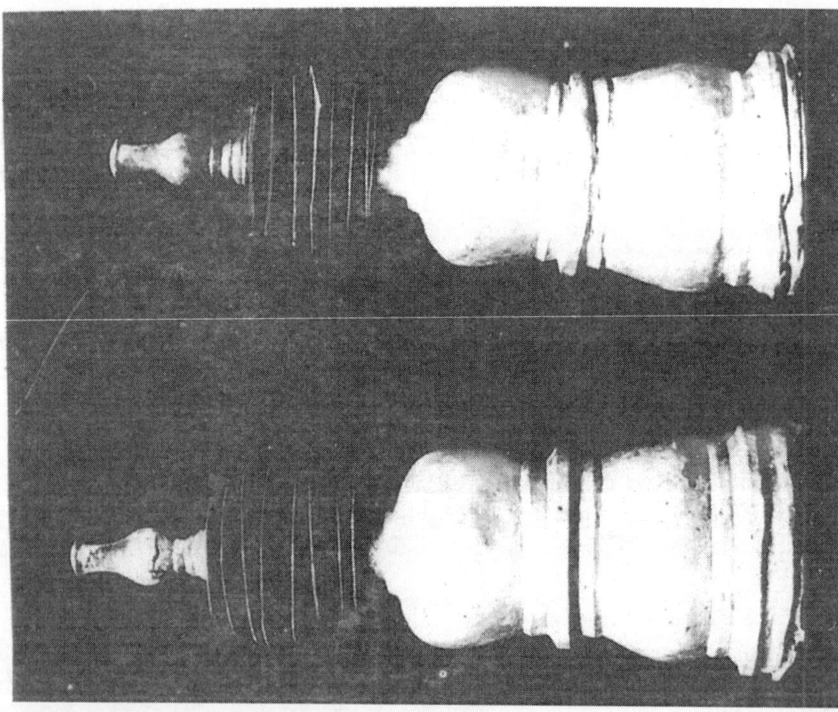

[74]

[75]

[76]

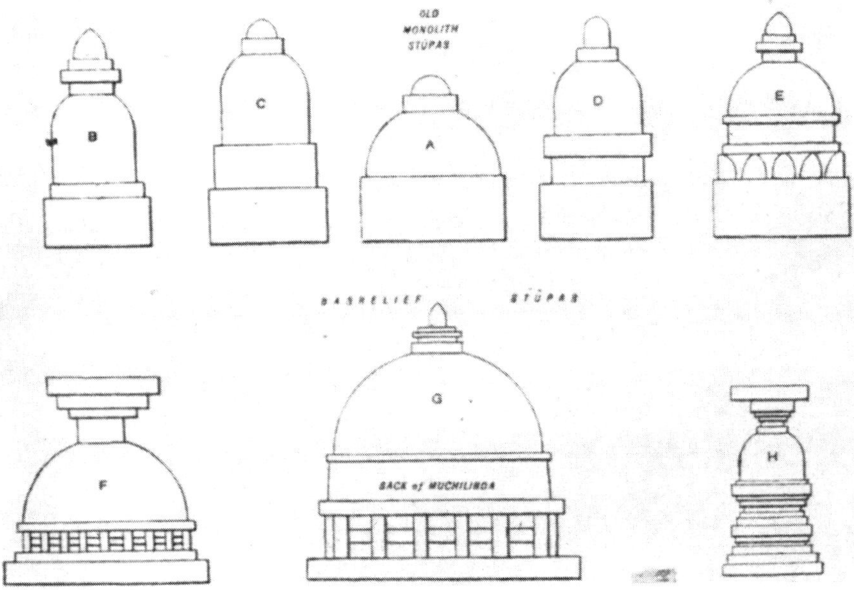
OLD MONOLITH STŪPAS
B
C
A
D
E
BASRELIEF STŪPAS
F
G
BACK of MUCHILINDA
H

[77]

[78]

[79]

[80]

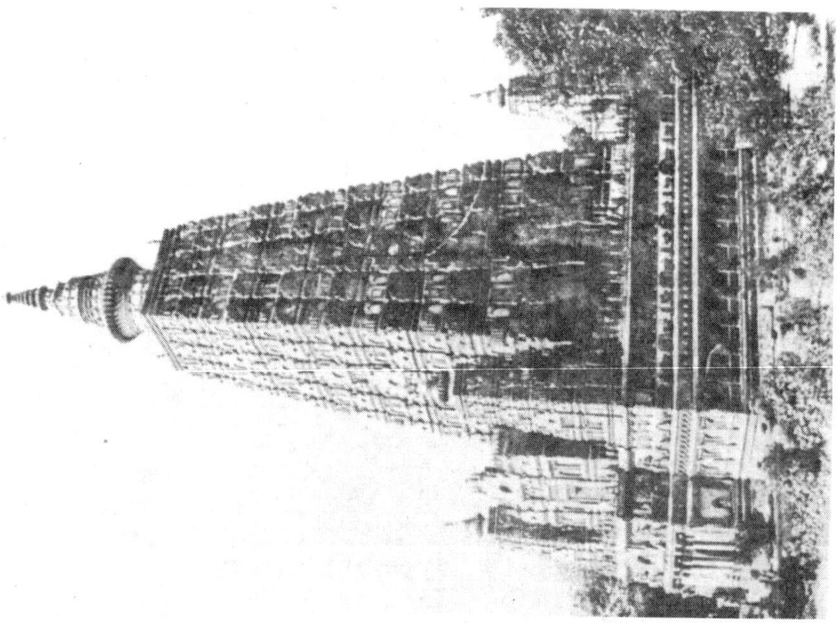

[81]

82]

[83]

⑦

[84]

[85]

TYPES OF SIKHARAS (TOWERS) OF TEMPLES IN THE NORTHERN OR INDO-ARYAN STYLE

45

[87]

[88

[89]

[90]

[91]

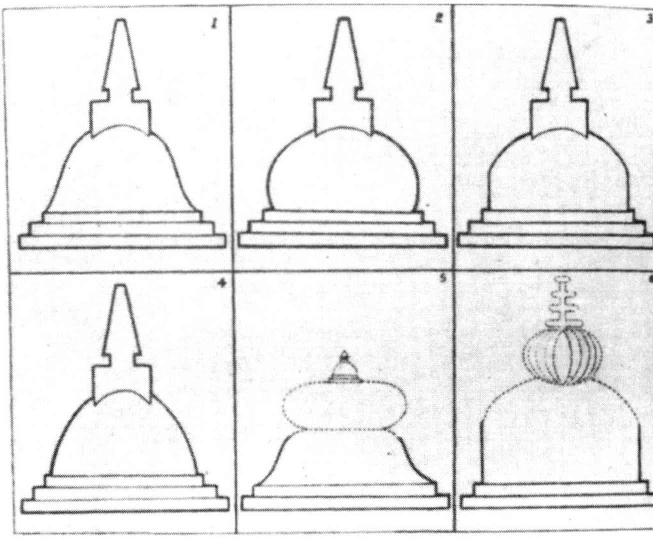

[92]

[93]

[94]

[95]

[96]

[97]

[98]

[99]

[100]

[101]

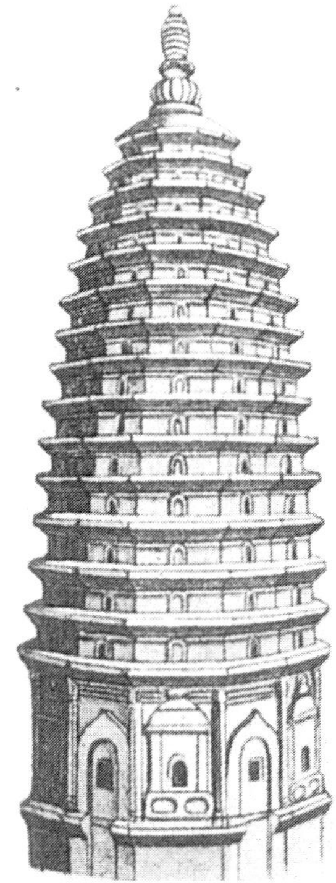

[102]

[103]

[104]

[105]

[106]

[107]

[108]

[109]

[110]

[III]

1

2

3

4

5

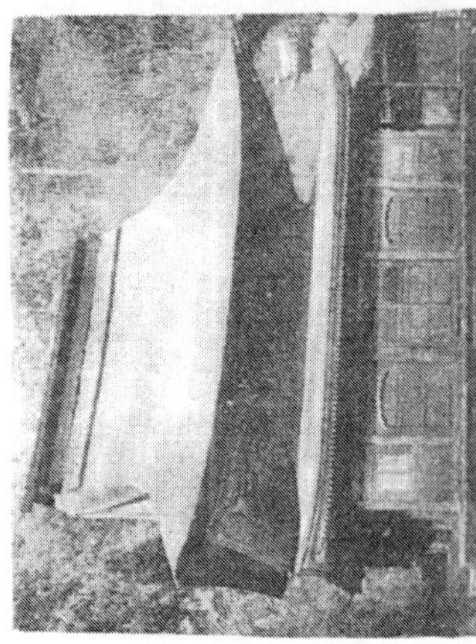

6

1

2

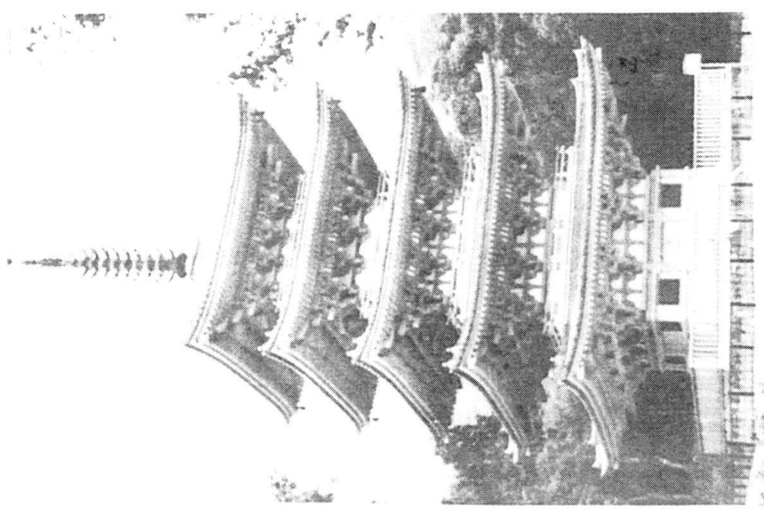
3

4

5

[112]

1. Various types of Dvāravatī stupa. After stone models and bas-reliefs in the National Museum, Bangkok.

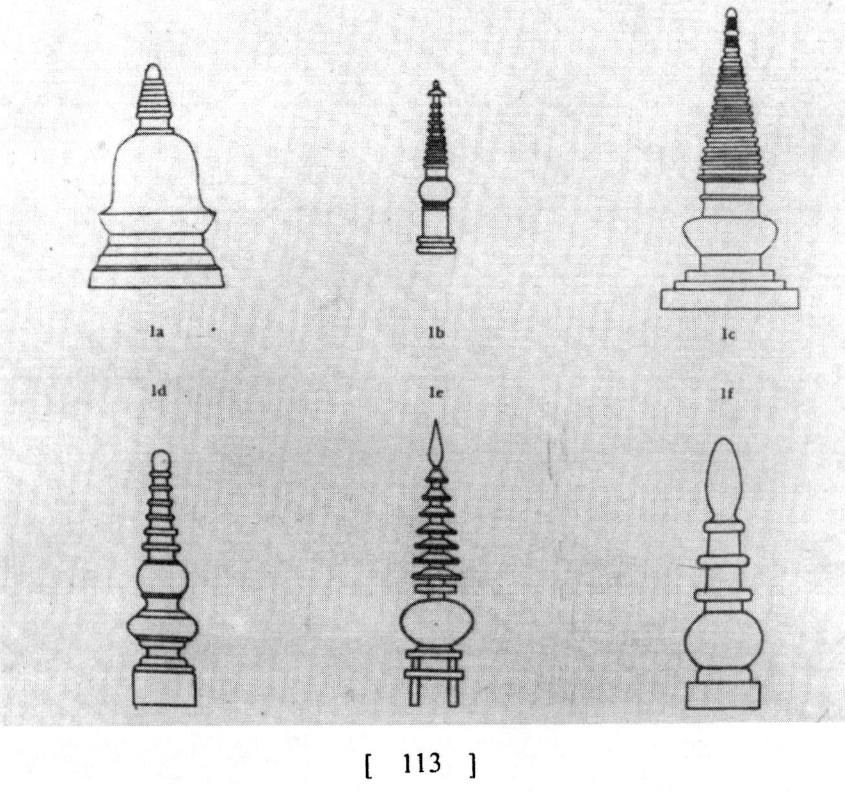

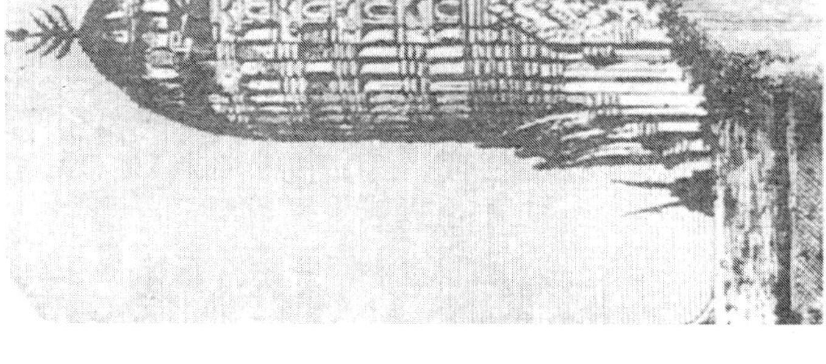

[114]

[115]

[116]

[117]

[118]

[119]

1

2

3

4

5

6

[120]

[121]

[122]

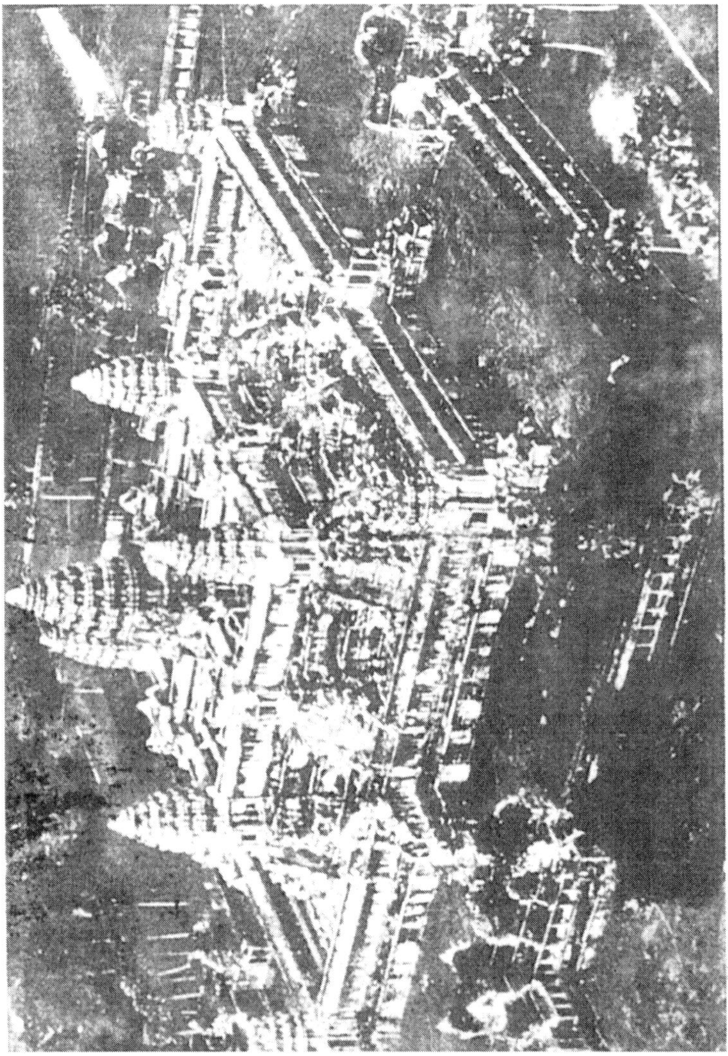

[123]

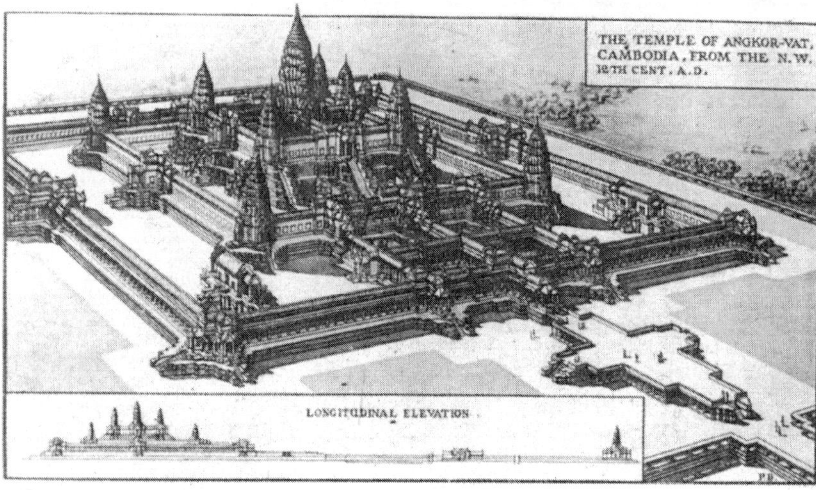
THE TEMPLE OF ANGKOR-VAT, CAMBODIA, FROM THE N.W. 12TH CENT. A.D.
LONGITUDINAL ELEVATION

[124]

[125]

[126]

[127]

[128]

[129]

[130]

[131]

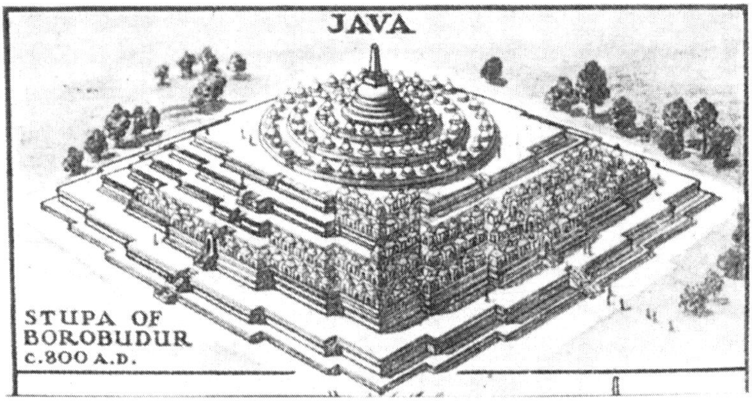

[132]

[133]

[134]

[135]

A Shrine at the ancient Buddhist university at Nalanda, India.

[136]

Ancient pagoda at Phnom Penh, Cambodia.

[137]

[138]